Lorcán Ó Tuathail
Drámadóir Mhaigh Cuilinn

Nollaig Mac Congáil
eagarthóir

Lorcán Ó Tuathail
Drámadóir Mhaigh Cuilinn

ARLEN
HOUSE

Lorcán Ó Tuathail
Drámadóir Mhaigh Cuilinn

Foilsithe in 2018 ag
ARLEN HOUSE
42 Grange Abbey Road
Baldoyle, Dublin 13, Ireland
Fón/Facs: 00 353 86 8207617
Ríomhphost: arlenhouse@gmail.com
arlenhouse.blogspot.com

Dáileoirí idirnáisiúnta
SYRACUSE UNIVERSITY PRESS
621 Skytop Road, Suite 110
Syracuse, NY 13244–5290
Fón: 315–443–5534/Facs: 315–443–5545
Ríomhphost: supress@syr.edu
www.syracuseuniversitypress.syr.edu

ISBN 978–1–85132–170–4, bog

Tá Arlen House buíoch de
Chlár na Leabhar Gaeilge
agus d'Fhoras na Gaeilge

Foras na Gaeilge

Clár

RÉAMHRÁ
LORCÁN Ó TUATHAIL (1870–1909)

Tháinig borradh mór faoin taighde atá á dhéanamh ar luathstair na hAthbheochana le blianta beaga anuas. Más mall is mithid. Is léir de bharr an taighde chéanna nach bhfuilimid ar an eolas go hiomlán faoin ghluaiseacht sin ná faoi na daoine iomadúla a raibh lámh acu inti. Táthar ag cur lenár gcuid eolais in aghaidh na bliana de bharr go bhfuil méadú ag teacht ar líon na dtaighdeoirí agus na réimsí taighde a bhíonn faoi scrúdú acu, go bhfuiltear ag teacht ar fhoinsí úra eolais agus go bhfuil teacht níos éasca ar fhoinsí taighde.

Sa taighde a rinneadh go dtí seo, rinneadh faillí in imeachtaí agus i ndaoine tábhachtacha thall is abhus ó cheann ceann na tíre i stair na hAthbheochana agus ní mór an scéal sin a leigheas. Caithfear cuimhneamh ar na daoine sin ach go háirithe a rinne a gcion féin ar son na hAthbheochana agus nach gcuimhnítear mórán orthu sa lá atá inniu ann. Duine acu sin an Gaillmheach Lorcán Ó Tuathail a ligeadh i ndearmad ó tharla go bhfuair sé bás go measartha óg ag tús an chéid seo caite, nach raibh ról lárnach, náisiúnta aige i gConradh na Gaeilge, nár foilsíodh mórán leis i gcaitheamh a shaoil agus nach raibh aon sliocht air a chuirfeadh daoine ar an eolas faoi. Is mithid anois féacháil le scéal a bheatha a ríomh agus a ról i scéal na hAthbheochana a rianú chomh fada agus is féidir.[1]

Rugadh Lorcán[2] Ó Tuathail cóngarach do shráidbhaile Mhaigh Cuilinn i gcontae na Gaillimhe sa bhliain 1870.[3]

> An t-aon Erwin L. Toole a rugadh i Maigh Cuilinn timpeall 1871 ba é Erwin Lawrence Toole é a rugadh i mBaile na hAille[4] ar 9 Eanáir 1870.[5] Ba iad James Toole, talmhaí, agus Brigid McDonagh, a thuismitheoirí.[6]

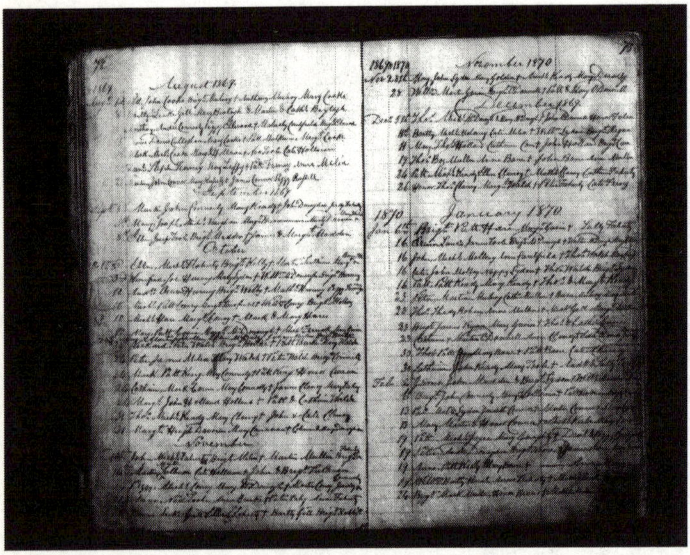

Ceantar láidir Gaeltachta a bhí i gceantar Mhaigh Cuilinn sa naoú haois déag agus mar sin a bhí go ceann na mblianta ina dhiaidh sin. Ní hamháin sin ach bhí spiorad maith Gaeilge sa cheantar mar is léir ó na tuairiscí seo a leanas ag tagairt do bhlianta fada i ndiaidh bhreith Lorcáin:

> *The Moycullen Branch reports 120 members. The parish priest preaches in Irish; the Rosary and other prayers are said in Irish in*

the church every Sunday. Irish is the principal medium between the residents. The language is also taught in the National Schools.[7]
One hundred per cent of the inhabitants speak Irish in Moycullen.[8]

Mar theist bhreise ar an áit ó thaobh na Gaeilge de, is ansin a rugadh an scríbhneoir agus an t-iriseoir Tomás Bairéad (1893–1973),[9] an tOllamh le Gaeilge Tomás Ó Raghallaigh (1883–1966)[10] agus, níos cóngaraí dár lá féin, an scríbhneoir, léachtóir agus fear béaloidis Pádraic Breathnach. Ceantar a bhí ann freisin a bhí ar maos sa sean-am sa traidisiún béil.[11]

Ina Mhúinteoir i Scoil Theach na mBocht

Níl aon eolas faoi óige Lorcáin ach gur bhain sé a cháilíochtaí múinteoireachta amach i gColáiste Phádraig, Droim Conrach. Luadh a ainm go poiblí den chéad uair go moltach mar mhúinteoir i dTeach na mBocht i gcathair na Gaillimhe sa bhliain 1896 sa sliocht seo a leanas, post a bhí aige le blianta roimhe sin agus go ceann blianta ina dhiaidh sin, is cosúil:

The Workhouse Schools

We direct the attention of our readers to the very able letter on Workhouse teachers contributed to our paper this week by the writer of the articles on 'The National Teachers and Primary Education' which has been for some weeks past appearing in our columns.[12] *Mr. Curtin makes out a really good case, and we have no doubt the guardians will give the matter their best consideration when an application will be made to them on next Wednesday by* ***Mr. O'Toole, the very efficient teacher at the Galway workhouse****. Should the local Guardians agree to the request for an increased salary to* ***a most deserving and respected officer*** *it will be no burden on the ratepayers as such will come from the Treasury. Favourable action in this matter on the part of the Guardians if confirmed by the Local Government Board will secure in some measure a fitting reward of merit. Indeed the constant and multifarious duties of a workhouse teacher are no enviable ones. We heartily commend Mr. O'Toole's reasonable claims to the notice of our Galway Guardians.*[13]

Is léir go raibh spéis ag Lorcán in Athbheochan na Gaeilge sna blianta sin óir tuairiscíodh ar *Fáinne an Lae* (16/7/1898, 11) gur thug L. O'Toole, Esq. N.T., síntiús 5s do chiste na feise i nGaillimh.

San iris sin ar 13 Aibreán 1901 freisin tuairiscíodh go raibh Scoil Theach na mBocht, cathair na Gaillimhe, ar na scoileanna a bhuaigh duaiseanna an Chliabhraigh[14] agus gurbh é Lorcán Ó Tuathail an múinteoir sa scoil sin.[15] Sin teist bhreise ar a fheabhas mar mhúinteoir agus a thiomantas don Ghaeilge.

I nDaonáireamh 1901 luaitear go raibh Erwin L. Toole ag múineadh agus ag cur faoi i dTeach na mBocht, Townpark, i gcathair na Gaillimhe. Bhí sé tríocha bliain d'aois ag an am.

> *Erwin L. Toole. Male. Schoolmaster. R.C.*
>
> *Read and Write English and Irish. Not married.*
>
> *Resident of a house 10.1 in Town Parks (Galway West Urban, Galway).*

An bhliain dár gcionn is é an seoladh a thug Lorcán, agus é ag tabhairt trí scillinge do Chiste na Teanga, Bóthar an Chaisleáin Nua, Gaillimh.[16]

Ina Dhrámadóir

Le linn dó a bheith ag múineadh i nGaillimh, is léir gur chuir sé spéis sa drámaíocht. Foilsíodh a dhráma 'Lá an Chíosa' ar *An Claidheamh Soluis*, 24 Deireadh Fómhair 1903 go 5 Nollaig 1903. Níor foilsíodh an dráma céanna i bhfoirm leabhair riamh gí gur léiríodh é thall is abhus.[17] Caithfear cuimhneamh go raibh drámaí Gaeilge agus traidisiún na drámaíochta Gaeilge lag go maith san am sin ar fud na hÉireann ach cuireadh fáilte roimh an dráma seo. An t-aon traidisiún drámaíochta a bhí maíte ar Ghaillimh sular scríobhadh an dráma seo, na drámaí a scríobh de hÍde faoi thionchar Lady Gregory agus *An Dochtúir* le Séamus Ó Beirn as Tamhain a léiríodh den chéad uair sa bhliain 1902 agus go rialta ina dhiaidh sin. Shamhlóinn, in áit ar nós chathair na Gaillimhe, go raibh Lorcán eolach go maith ar shaothar drámatúil an triúir sin nuair a thug sé faoi dhrámaí dá chuid féin a scríobh.

Bhain an dráma 'Lá an Chíosa' le téama a bhí comhaimseartha go leor ag an am, ceist na dtiarnaí talaimh agus an leatrom cíosa a d'fhulaing tionóntaí. Foilsíodh an cuntas seo a leanas ar an dráma.

THE RENT DAY by E.L. O'Toole[18]

The production of a drama in Irish, written for Irish speakers by one of themselves, is a step in the right direction. There is no imitation here, either in construction or in language. Mr. O'Toole's language is most idiomatic, and his treatment of his subject most dramatic. It is his first effort in play-writing and is, perhaps, the best play in Irish written so far. The rent day is a very characteristic event in Irish country life. To the poor, hard-working tenants it is the event of the year – the turning-point round which hangs the fortunes of themselves and their families. Will they be able to scrape together the rent or not? That is the great question for them. If they can do so they may live yet another year in the homes of their fathers; if they cannot, they, with their wives and little ones, are flung out on the roadside to starve or emigrate. The rent day, let us hope, will soon be a thing of the past. It is well therefore that Mr. O'Toole has described it so well for the information and delectation of future generations. From start to finish his play is full of incident and life. It never flags. The characters of the different tenants as they pay their rents is well portrayed; from the independent Black John who tells the master: 'Maybe it's thankful to you you expect us to be that you leave us alive at all,' to poor Ready Mick who, owing to the sickness of his wife and children, has not the wherewithal to pay. The intercession of the landlord's wife, the detections of the lying, cunning, scheming bailiff, and the answering of the three questions by the village trickster, lead up to the climax – the repentance of the landlord for the evil which, under the bailiff's influence, he had unwittingly done, and his determination to make amends by selling out and dividing his own land among his tenants. The country people in the audience were delighted with the play. I heard one of them, a very old man, say: 'At races, or fair or patron I never seen anything so good and I'll go to none of them in future.' The verdict of the Irish speakers, those for whom Mr. O'Toole wrote, was unmistakable. They were in ecstacies over it. They had never been appealed to so before. Mr. O'Toole is young yet and it is a very promising thing that his first production should be so good. I am sure he will improve and delight us with many other and even better dramas.

Connacht should be the centre of the new literary movement. It is fitted to be so in every way and perhaps it will be when we shake off our long-worn lethargy. The 'battle-challenge' has 'pierced the sky'; it is time we bethought us of 'leaping into life.'

Tomás Breathnach[19]

Tháinig Lorcán os comhair an phobail sa bhliain sin freisin ar chúis eile ar fad nuair a scríobh sé alt ar fhile fadsaolach Chonamara, mar atá, Colm de Bhailís a raibh aithne aige air. Tharraing a chuntas a bheagán nó a mhórán aighnis mar is léir ón alt agus ón chomhfhreagras a lean é.

COLUM WALLACE THE VETERAN IRISH POET
THE 'PATRIARCH OF GORUMNA'

The most remarkable figure in Gaelic Ireland just now is Colum Wallace, the Gorumna poet, now living hale and hearty at the extraordinary age of 107, and who up to a few weeks ago had been for some time an inmate of Oughterard Workhouse. It is a painful commentary on the neglect and decay of our grand old Irish tongue, that Colum, who added a lustre to Irish poetry, should ever have been forced to seek refuge in the last home of the destitute.

I asked an old Gaeilgeoir a few days ago, did he know Colum Wallace and he said no, but that he heard about him! 'And where is the person,' he added, 'who didn't hear about him? Sure there was never any satisfaction at a wedding or pattern without some of Colum's seandáns being sung there, still no one was fully satisfied without Colum himself being there to sing them, for no one could sing them as well as he.' If he never wrote but 'Cúirt an tSrutháin Bhuí' he would deserve the gratitude of all who appreciate the beauty of our old Irish songs. Though not yet published, it is said to be the best Irish piece ever composed. It is a rare treat to hear the author himself give 'Cúirt an tSrutháin Bhuí'[20] *in grand traditional style. One goes away bewailing the thought that he has left no heirs to his genius and that we have few like him in Ireland now for with him goes the last of the real old Irish poets.*

Colum was two years of age when the French landed in Killala in 1798, yet old age sits so lightly on him that he seems to be no more than 70, while his spirits are as gay as those of a schoolboy. These circumstances may have given rise to a dispute about his age a few months ago. Accordingly, reference was made to the Parish Register in Gorumna when it was found that Colum was born on May 2nd, 1796. 'Is it true,' said I, 'that you are one hundred and seven years of age?' 'It is true,' he replied. 'It is wonderful indeed, thanks be to God! However, I did my own part of it. I never abused my health and I always kept sober, and sure there is a great deal in that.'

When the pitiful circumstances connected with the closing days of Colum's long career was reported to the Executive of the Gaelic League, that body was not slow in coming to his rescue. They removed him from the Workhouse and from the ignominy of a pauper's grave, and though the sum collected for his maintenance is still limited, they rely on the friends of the Irish Language Movement to secure for this poor victim of unprovided age, an allowance that will enable him to live in comfort during the remainder of his days, even though his patriarchal age be prolonged for many years.

The prophecy that Colum Wallace would die immediately after leaving the Workhouse has happily not been fulfilled and is not likely to be. He appears twenty years younger now than he was when confined within the grim walls of that institution. When asked how did he like the change of air, Colum replied: 'Oh, I feel like a person after coming out of hell.' However, he had nothing but praise for the officers of the house but, being of a sensitive disposition, he felt that the rough character of the Workhouse were no company for him.

Up to the age of 50, Colum plied the craft of a fisherman, with much success. Strange to say, he relinquished this calling for the occupation of a sawyer which he followed for thirty years after. He worked in nearly every county in Ireland and never left the country.[21]

Tugadh freagra air sin ina dhiaidh sin.

COLUMB WALLACE: The 'Patriarch of Gorumna'

To the Editor of the Galway Observer*:*

Sir,

On last issue of your excellent paper there is an interesting article **re** *the above. The writer, in his zeal and admiration for his hero, is somewhat in error when he states that Columb is the author of that clever popular song 'Cuirt an Farothain Bhuidhe [= Cúirt an tSrutháin Bhuí],' which was composed by Meichel Deramid Cloherty, of Insh-a-ganna, Lettercalla, on the rugged shore of the beautiful Bay of Kilkerrin. When Cloherty's muse became fatigued and exhausted, an old, lame man called Shaun Bockagh Gorham, of Letterard, in the parish of Carna, took up the lyre, which Cloherty's muse had laid aside, and he added six or seven other verses to it. The 'Sruffaun Bhuidhe' is a mountain stream or rivulet near Lettermore or Lettercalla, on whose bank some squatter built a sod cabin, about eight feet square and five feet high; so Cloherty lampooned and exaggerated it, saying it far exceeded in beauty of design any castle or mansion of ancient or modern times, just as Sweeney exaggerated the wedding of Peggy O'Hara, who* *was only a servant girl to one of the Bodkins, of Omey Island.*

Some years since I paid a visit to the Bard, Cloherty. I was accompanied by a very distinguished Irish-American scholar, Mr. Jeremia Curtin, Professor of Languages, Harvard College, Washington, a famous writer and translator, and we came suddenly on the Bard, who was old but hardy, basking in the sun beneath a fence. The aged minstrel was at the same time nursing a baby in a most skilful, matronly manner, and he informed us his son and daughter-in-law were out on the high seas kelp-gathering. So said this aged poet: 'I am minding the house and taking care of the 'chilther.'' Gorham was a match for him in every way. To me they seemed to be as clever Bards as any who ever appeared in ancient Erin. They may be equalled, but could hardly be excelled. They, I fear, were the last of their class, the poor old Homers who were respected by those who spoke Irish, while they were despised and laughed at by those who spoke English. Alas! They lie slumbering in some obscure corner, with the rank nettles blooming above them; there they lie neglected and forgotten. – SKIRDA-MORE[22]

Tarraingíodh daoine eile isteach sa chonspóid ansin mar a tharlaíonn go minic ar ócáidí mar sin.

Colum Wallace

The Patriarch of Gorumna

97, Stephen's Green,

Dublin 24th August, 1903

To the Editor of the Galway Observer*:*

Dear Sir,

Your correspondent, 'Skirdamore' has not got hold of the true origin of Colum Wallace's 'Court of the Yellow Stream.' As every man, woman and child in Gorumna knows, it was Colum himself who composed it. I wrote it down in 1900, partly from Colum's own lips, and partly from the dictation of Mr. Patrick MacDonagh, J.P., and Mr. Dermot O'Loughlin, of Gortumna. This version will be found in

__Celtia__ for October 1902. I omitted the last three verses in my possession, one of which was made by Colum and contained a reference to Mr. Cloherty, of Lettercalla, while the other two were made by the latter. Mr. Cloherty's poems are well known in Gorumna, and it is equally well known there that he never claimed to have composed the main portion of 'Cúirt an tSrutháin Bhuí.' This song, when sung by Gorumna people, is always interspersed with 'deir an Wallasach' – the conventional way of preserving the name of the author.

Yours faithfully,

E.E. Fournier.[23]

Ní raibh Lorcán róshásta gur tugadh bréagach dó, áfach.[24]

To the Editor of the Galway Observer:

Sir,

I have read in the last issue of your widely-circulated journal an extraordinary letter about Colum Wallace, the veteran Irish poet, from an anonymous scribbler, who, in his feeble and cowardly attempt to write down the fame of the aged bard of Gorumna, conceals his identity behind 'Skirda More.'

The pseudonym is peculiarly suggestive: in the minds of the average Gael, it probably conjures up rather unpleasant recollections of those big, greedy 'sgiorrtans,' or parasites, who, for centuries, have prospered on the decay of the Celtic tongue.

'Twas fading, oh, 'twas fading, like the leaves upon the trees,
While the 'sgiorrtans' and the Seoiníns stood quite content at ease.

I am not aware whether 'Skirda-More' is one of the genuine 'sgiorrtans,' but, judging from his vulgar epistle, he evidently has no knowledge of Irish. May I, therefore, infer, from his own hypothesis, that in days gone by he was one of those 'lau-de-daus' who hated and despised those who knew no English.

His significant sneer about my 'enthusiastic admiration' for my 'hero' will doubtless be fully appreciated; so also will his 'fear' that 'Deramid' Cloherty and 'Shawn Brockagh' Gorham, as he is pleased to call the 'rivals' of old Colum, were the last of their class, and that with them has gone for ever all hope of redeeming our historic past.

Now, Sir, 'Skirda-More's' excuse for bringing himself into a controversy about Irish poets and poetry, about which he has a good deal yet to learn, appears to lie in the statement made by me in a previous issue of the __Observer__, namely, that Colum Wallace is the author of a beautiful Irish poem entitled 'Cúirt an tSrutháin Bhuí', to which I still and will adhere and in support of which I have ample proof from persons who knew Colum well and whose verdict as to the authorship of 'An Sruthán' was not influenced by partiality towards one poet or another. At the same time I consider it a mere waste of powder to reply to the attacks of an individual whose ignorance of the simplest rules of orthography is as patent as the absurdity of his theories about the Bards of Gorumna Island. Why, the idea of a warrior going into the field of battle, armed with a pop-gun, pales into insignificance before his. 'Skirda-More's' necessary arms and ammunition are quite simple: all he requires in order to demolish me is the ***Claidheamh Soluis*** *and a good Irish dictionary in one hand, with a copious supply of Hyde and O'Growney in the other.*

Is mise,

Údar ***Lá an Chíosa.***[25]

Is cinnte nach raibh Lorcán sásta fanacht ina thost ar an ócáid. Is spéisiúil an rud é go dtugann sé 'údar Lá an Chíosa' air féin seachas a ainm féin, comhartha go bhfuil aithne air agus roinnt aitheantais faighte aige mar údar an dráma sin ag an am.

Mar eolas breise faoi phost Lorcáin i dTeach na mBocht ag an am, tuairiscíodh ar *An Claidheamh Soluis* (13/2/1904, 5) gur aontaigh na *Galway Guardians to make special payments for the teaching of Irish in the Workhouse Schools.*

Tháinig an dara dráma ó Lorcán tamall ina dhiaidh sin agus dráma, arís, nár foilsíodh riamh i bhfoirm leabhair nó nár cuireadh i gcló. Ó tharla nach bhfuil fáil ar an dráma, ní miste cuntas comhaimseartha a thabhairt air anseo, go háirithe ó tá ceisteanna ann faoi údar agus stair léirithe an dráma.

GALWAY PLAY PRODUCED IN LONDON

(To the Editor of the Galway Express)

Sir – I do not often worry you with a letter. I hope, on this account, you will print the enclosed. There are a few Galwegians who will read it with unusual interest, but I can only vouch for a few.

Early in the present year Leabhras Ó Tuathail and Thomas Breathnach, both Galway men, collaborated in the writing of a play in Irish for the last Galway Feis.[26] *They called the play* **An Cleamhnas**. *Your Irish speakers know what* **An Cleamhnas** *means. Through some hitch or another, however,* **An Cleamhnas** *was not produced at the Feis. Dr. Hyde wrote one on the very same subject, and his was staged instead.*

In the meantime, an exile from Galway, 'earning English gold' in London, came along and saw **An Cleamhnas**. *He there and then decided that it would 'go' splendidly before an Irish audience here. After a little negotiation, some letter-writing, and innumerable rehearsals,* **An Cleamhas** *– renamed by us* **Cleamhnas Chrustóra** *for convenience of reference – was produced here on Thursday evening last to a fairly crowded house of splendid enthusiasts. We took the Middleton Hall, Almeida Street, Islington, N., for the purpose, and your readers will be interested to hear that the stage alone of this hall is almost as big as Galway Town Hall. This was our cast:* [luaitear ainmneacha na n-aisteoirí, ina measc P. O'Conroy, Galway.[27]]

Cleamhnas Chrustóra *was, of course, written for a Galway audience. The scene is placed in Galway, and, need it be added, the language used is peculiarly local Irish in phraseology. Yet this did not in the least interfere with the successful presentation of the play. Most of the cast, as will be seen, are from Munster, and of course speak with the Munster accent. Well, in rehearsing the play we mutually agreed that each member of the cast would speak the Irish that seemed to him most natural. If you were a Kerryman, put the Kerry 'blas' on your speech; if a Galwayman, put on the Galway accent, and so on. This worked admirably only, of course, it gave the play a most interesting aspect from the point of view of the authors. I ought, indeed, to say at this juncture that* **Cleamhnas Chrustóra** *did not suffer much, if at all in being treated in the way I have indicated. To resume, the play was produced on Thursday evening last, and we had a good house in spite of the fact that the affair was not well advertised. It would do your average Galwegian good to see how an Irish gathering in London supports and applauds anything that is genuinely racy of the soil, anything that makes for the social or the intellectual good of their country. I am speaking, of course, of Irishmen who are Irish Irelanders and do not apologise for the fact.*

Taken all round our cast was a good one, particularly Paddy O'Conroy, whose biting home thrusts at the Crustóir were worth going a long way to hear.

In brief, the plot of the play was to the following effect:

The happy-go-lucky, thriftless, Galway farmer, Tadhg, returns from the fair, 'magaleor', and tells Maighréad, his careful, foreseeing housewife, that he has spent the day with Crustóir, with whom he has arranged to come that evening and make a match with Brighid, Tadhg's sole remaining joy. Maighréad does not seem to take kindly to the idea of the Crustóir as a son-in-law, and as for poor Brighid who has already handed over her heart to Seaghan Mhichíl, she steadfastly refuses to even see the old cripple. However, Maighréad assumes a more complacent manner when Tadhg tells how the Crustóir's 'wealth' may be the immediate means of saving them from their threatened eviction on the morrow. The Crustóir is due at 8.00 so Tadhg sets off to meet him. Meanwhile Domhnall Glic, the ready-tongued, 'drops in' and Crustóir's short-comings and other traits are discussed with great freedom and hardly much respect. Presently Tadhg returns in great spirits with the Crustóir and a friend of the latter. The match-making is got through – Brighid being purposely absent 'ill' for the occasion. There are a few songs and then Tadhg, with his eye to 'business,' asks the Crustóir for the money. The latter, not having it on him, is sent home for it. While the crusty old cripple is away, Seaghan Mhichíl enters in company with an uncle, Micheál Mór, just returned from America. Tadhg will not have any truck with a raw youth like Seaghan 'who has not the second bit to put in his mouth.' When, however, Seaghan explains that he is no longer a poor farmer's poor son, thanks to his rich uncle, Micheál Mór, Tadhg 'thaws' off a good deal. When Tadhg finally discovers in Micheál an old school and playmate, Tadhg suddenly becomes enthusiastic over the prospect of Brighid's marriage with Seaghan Mhichíl. Brighid is there and then 'fixed up' anew. It can be quickly surmised what happens when the Crustóir again appears on the scene. Micheál Mór's description of life in America – that 'hell with the lid off' – is a capital anti-emigration argument that would do a lot of good if delivered at every crossroads in the diocese of Galway.

It will be seen from the plot that there was good room for fun and diversion, and the serious, propagandist side of the story was not forgotten. The audience, most diligent students of the language, and a good proportion of them native speakers, followed the play with admirable keenness. No point was lost, and the general verdict was that **Cleamhnas Chrustóra** *provided a good hour's fun and enjoyment.*

It seems a pity that these two Galway men should have to send their work over here to London for production. I understand that when **An**

> ***Dochtúir*** *was staged at the Town Hall recently by the Tawin players, the house was hardly half-filled, and yet this same play drew densely-packed houses in Dublin on three successive nights.*
>
> *I hope the fact of* ***Cleamhnas Chrustóra*** *being, now, 'a London success,' will assure it a hearty welcome should it ever be staged in Galway. I think it would make a capital piece for inclusion in the Temperance Hall St. Stephen's Night entertainment. It only occupies an hour and the Irish is most simple and very 'local,' if I may use the word.*
>
> *Thanking you beforehand for publishing this long screed.*
>
> *Yours truly,*
>
> *Carraig Bhaidhte, London, Samhain, 23, 1903.*[28]

In alt eile tugadh an chreidiúint ar fad do Thomás Breathnach mar údar an dráma.[29] Is cosúil, áfach, gur chomhúdair ar an dráma iad.

> *At the prize-winners' concert in the evening, the Galway Branch produced a new play in Irish by Mr. O'Toole and Dr. T. Walsh, B.A., Oranmore, entitled* ***Cleamhnas na Chrustóir*** *a satire on the system of match-making prevailing in many parts of Ireland.*[30]

Bhí a dhintiúir dhrámata bainte amach ag Lorcán Ó Tuathail mar sin nuair a scríobh sé an dráma is cáiliúla dá chuid, mar atá, *An Deoraidhe,* sa bhliain 1904, an t-aon dráma dá chuid a foilsíodh i bhfoirm leabhair. Tuairiscíodh ar *An Claidheamh Soluis*[31] gur léiríodh é ar an 17 Márta, 1904 i nGaillimh:

> *In the evening Mr O'Toole's new play* ***An Deoraidhe*** *was produced in the Town Hall before an audience which packed every part of the building from the front seats to the top gallery. An Irish concert followed. The entertainment was, from every standpoint, the most successful yet given by the Gaelic League in Galway.*

Tugadh léirithe eile dó gan mhoill thall is abhus.[32] D'fhoilsigh Conradh na Gaeilge *An Deoraidhe*: dráma in aghaidh imeachta thar sáile, 1906 agus cuireadh an dara heagrán amach roimh dheireadh na bliana.[33] Scríobh An Craoibhín sa réamhrá:

> Chonaic mé *An Deoraidhe* i nGaillimh anuraidh agus is iomdha gáire do bhain sé asam. Bhí greann agus brón ann agus bhí teagasc slán folláin ann. Gaeilge bhreá so-léite do bhí ann, freisin. Ba mhaith liom é a fheiscint mar leabhar le léamh ins gach aon scoil agus dhéanfadh sé maith mór. Dhéanfadh sé maith ar dhá bhealach; ag múineadh Gaeilge coitinne na tíre do na páistí agus ag cur in iúl dóibh go mb'fhearr fanúint san mbaile ná dul go dtí an tOileán Úr.

Bhí ceist na himirce ar cheann de na hábhair ar dhírigh Conradh na Gaeilge aird uirthi go láidir arís is arís eile agus ní hiontas gur baineadh úsáid as téama na himirce i saothair luatha na hAthbheochana. Féach, ar an téad seo, Philip O'Leary, *The Prose Literature of the Gaelic Revival 1881–1921: Ideology and Innovation* (The Pennsylvania State University Press, 1994) 141 ff. agus Regina Uí Chollatáin, *An Claidheamh Soluis agus Fáinne an Lae 1899–1932* (Cois Life, 2004) 77–8. Ní Conradh na Gaeilge amháin a bhí buartha faoin imirce ach an eaglais is lucht gnó, polaiteoirí agus lucht talmhaíochta, rud a d'fhág an imirce mar ábhar cainte agus díospóireachta go minic ar nuachtáin is irisí.[34] Mar shampla, *The Anti-Emigration Society was formed on 25/5/1903 at a meeting at 6 D'Olier Street, Dublin, the object of the association being to combat emigration, especially emigration from the Irish Speaking districts.*[35]

Luaitear freisin 'Ban-Laoch na hÉireann' mar dhráma eile de chuid Lorcáin ach níl fáil air agus ní fios ar foilsíodh é in aon áit nó ar léiríodh é. Tá an deacracht chéanna ag baint lena dhráma *Dónall Diaganta*. Is cinnte gur scríobhadh é ag tús an chéid seo caite ach níor foilsíodh é, nó cuid de, go dtí i ndiaidh a bháis ar an *Connacht Tribune* (11/2/1911, 3, 4/3/1911, 8, 20/5/1911, 8, 3/6/11, 8).

Seo a leanas tuairisc chomhaimseartha ar léiriú den dráma *An Deoraidhe*.

THE EXILE

Synopsis of the Piece

Owing to the late hour on Friday night last at which the above [Connacht] Feis was brought to a close, we were unable to give a synopsis of that excellent Irish comedy **The Exile** *written by Mr. E.L. O'Toole, school teacher at the Galway Workhouse, and which won so much appreciation on its first introduction to the public on Wednesday night, that it was repeated by general request on the following Friday evening. The play was a representation of the anxiety for emigration which has taken hold of the Irish people for many years back, their impression being that they need only go to America or some other foreign land to realise a fortune. The comedy in question, of which we give a synopsis, portrays to life the manner in which the peasantry carry out what is known as 'An American Wake' on the eve of the emigration of any of the 'neighbours' from their district …*

Cait, a young Irish farmer's daughter, receives a letter from her sister abroad, full of the usual glowing accounts of America, where the proverbial milk and honey is flowing in abundance, and wherein is mentioned in particular the progress of Cait's former neighbours, especially one Mary Hynes, whose riches and grandeur are dazzling. Cait reads the amusing epistle to her father, who replies to the ridiculous statements contained therein with epithets of rebuke and sarcasm. Cait, however, maintains that everything stated in the letter about the fortunes of her erstwhile companion is perfectly true, and despite her father's protests resolves to go to America. The time-honoured 'American Wake' is then held, and all the neighbours previously invited drop in, bringing with them presents go leor, several of which are intended as souvenirs of the old land. Of all the gifts presented to the fair young emigrant, the most comical perhaps, was a sod of turf presented by an individual named 'Marcus na Gearc,' who, coming as he did without receiving any formal invitation, and under the pretence of bidding farewell to Cait, came really to look for a wife, a circumstance which induced Maurteen O'Roigeen, Cait's real lover, to refer to Marcus as the essence of meanness, which he did with effect, despite the protests of Marcus that it was owing to the scarcity of turf in America, and not through any stinginess on his part that he presented the young lady with such a seemingly ridiculous gift. Another neighbour, represented by Miss O'Halloran, Abbeygate Street, presented the young Cait with a home-made shawl, which was thoughtfully fitted on by Maurteen

O'Roigeen and highly appreciated by the handsome recipient. Other presents included an oat-meal cake, a blackthorn stick, and last but not least, a huge feather bed, presented by Mikeleen, the village authority, ably represented by Mr. A. McGlynn. A good deal of bantering took place about the feather bed, but Mikeleen effectively shouted that his gift represented the maximum of generosity shown to Cait that night. After a dispute between Maurteen and Marcus, the rival suitors, a dance is held, which is interrupted by the arrival on the scene of the supposed millionaire, Mary Hynes, whose wretched appearance fully belied the American fable letter in her regard. When she enters no-one recognises her, her appearance has changed so much. After a good deal of scrutiny her identity becomes known. She tells her story, a story of grinding toil and little joy, which is in striking contrast with the accounts of the phantom fortune stated in the letter.

... The play was brought to a conclusion by Cait accepting Maurteen as her future protector, which announcement sent the hunchback dancing with rage out of the house, the remainder of the company enjoying themselves with dancing and singing until daylight in the morning. The appearance of Miss Hynes, as above mentioned, changed the mind of Cait, and the happy union of hands with Maurteen changed the scene from the sadness of an American Wake to the happiness of an Irish wedding.[36]

An Deoraí

Arna chur amach i mBaile Átha Cliath

ag

Conradh na Gaeilge, M.H. Gill agus a mhac agus an Clóchumann (teoranta)

1905[37]

Thart ar an am seo freisin i nGaillimh, is léir nach raibh an claonadh in éadan na Gaeilge marbh ar fad óir tharla eachtra a bhain le ceapachán Thomáis Breathnach, dochtúir leighis, Gaeilgeoir agus an fear a scríobh dráma i gcomhar le Lorcán, agus a raibh baint ag Lorcán leis an scéal.

At a recent meeting a majority of the Galway Guardians elected an Irish-speaking doctor, Tomás Breathnach, to the dispensary at Oranmore. It was a lively meeting and the Irish movement was very much a live thing in its relation to this particular appointment.

There were two candidates and one, an Irish speaker, sent in his application in Irish. In addition to the Guardians, sixty out of sixty eight of whom were present, a large number of the public helped to overcrowd the room. The Chairman, Mr. P. Cannon, was an Englisher on this occasion, and apparently behaved as rudely as any Englisher might be expected to behave, and Mr. Murray remarked to him: 'Irish will be here after you.' Why there should have been any commotion, or even a division over the appointment, it is hard to see in face of the fact that the advertisement stated that preference would be given to an Irish speaker, and we presume that the medical qualifications of the two candidates were about the same. The Clerk of the Board was unable to read the Irish application of the Irish-speaking doctor; and Mr. Griffin proposed that anything that was not in plain English should not be read. This utterly anti-Irish remark, we read, caused a renewal of commotion and indeed we are not surprised that it did so. **Mr. O'Toole**, *the Workhouse Master, was asked to read the application of the Irish-speaking doctor, and the reading of it was interrupted by various exclamations, principally in Irish, and, we read, occasionally with such select English remarks as 'Shut your mouth there.' The application was as follows:-*

Tuaim, Oíche Shamhna, 1904.

A dhaoine uaisle,

Leis seo cuirim isteach ar an áit dochtúra atá anois folamh in Órán Mór. Tá mé ag cur chugaibh mo pháipéir & mo cháilíocht. Ón am a chuaigh mé tríd mo scrúdú déanach bhí mé i mo dhochtúir i nGort & in ospidéal Chontae na Gaillimhe. Tá mé in ann Gaeilge a labhairt go maith & tá súil agam nach ndéanfaidh sibh dearmad air sin nuair atá sibh ag cur an dochtúir isteach.

Mise le meas mór,

Tomás Breathnach (Thomas Walsh)

At the conclusion of the reading of the application there was great applause. On a division Dr. Walsh was elected by 32 votes to 27, one of the sixty Guardians present declining to vote.[38]

I mblianta luatha an chéid seo caite is léir go raibh Lorcán gníomhach i gcur chun cinn na Gaeilge ina scoil féin nó bhain cuid dá chuid daltaí an *Cleaver Book Prize*[39] sa bhliain 1905.

Lorcán Ua Tuathail, Scoil Tighe na mBocht, Gaillimh Gortrua
Prizes 1905 (Schools from Irish-speaking areas who entered)
Lorcán Ua Tuathail, Scoil Tighe na mBocht, Gaillimh[40]

Is léir freisin go raibh sé gníomhach i gConradh na Gaeilge nó luadh sa bhliain 1906 go raibh sé i láthair ag '*Meeting of delegates of Gaelic League Branches.*'[41]

Saothrú na Drámaíochta i nGaillimh

Bhí traidisiún láidir drámaíochta Gaeilge ag baint le Gaillimh ag tús an chéid seo caite agus bhí dlúthcheangal aige sin le lucht saothraithe na drámaíochta Béarla.[42] Ba í Lady Augusta Gregory an ceangal idir an dá dhream agus, ar bhealach, ba í máthair na drámaíochta Gaeilge í i ndáiríre. Murach a ceangal agus a caidreamh le Yeats agus de hÍde,[43] gan trácht ar dhreibhlín eile an *Irish Literary Theatre,* drochsheans go ndéanfaí an drámaíocht Ghaeilge a fhorbairt mar a rinneadh, go háirithe san Iarthar.[44]

> *Lady Gregory stated publicly that drama in Irish began with the Punch-and-Judy show performed by Hyde and Norma Borthwick for her schoolchildren's Christmas party at Coole in 1898.*[45]

Bíodh an ceart aici nó ná bíodh sa mhéid sin, bhí ról lárnach aici féin agus a comhluadar i spreagadh, i gcothú agus in oiliúint de hÍde mar dhrámadóir Gaeilge agus, ar ndóigh, bhí baint mhór ag de hÍde leis an *ILT* ó bunaíodh é.

> *His manuscripts were often revised following the critical readings which resulted in suggestions for revision from Yeats and Lady Gregory … or from George Moore and AE.*[46]

Rianaítear stair scríofa *Casadh an tSúgáin* mar seo a leanas i ndialann de hÍde, mar shampla:

28 August 1900	*Yeats set me writing a play on 'The Twisting of the Rope', and I wrote a good part of it from the scenario he drew up for me.*
29 August 1900	*Finishing 'The Twisting of the Rope'. Tired and a little unwell. Lady*

	Gregory gave me a bottle of champagne at dinner.
30 August 1900	*Martyn came to dinner. I read 'The Twisting of the Rope' to him yesterday and he was pleased with it.*
31 August 1900	*Yesterday and today I read 'The Twisting of the Rope' to Lady Gregory and she typed it in English from my dictation. A fine day. I wrote another little part of a play.*[47]

Is léir, áfach, ón taighde a rinneadh ar shíolrú agus ar éabhlóid roinnt drámaí eile le de hÍde agus Lady Gregory, chomh maith leis na leaganacha Béarla a rinneadh díobh, go gcaithfear creidiúint a thabhairt do thionchar agus do bhuanna éagsúla na beirte i gcruthú na ndrámaí céanna sin.[48] Mar shampla, deir Lady Gregory ina dialann: *'We [i.e. í féin agus Yeats] made the scenarios of 'Lost Saint' & 'Nativity' and a 'Fearful Dream' for Hyde.'*[49] An rud is mó atá ar shlí a ráite anseo agus ar fiú cuimhne a choinneáil air, gur bhain drámaí seo de hÍde, bíodh eithne an téama, forbairt an phlota nó láimhseáil an dráma i gcoitinne i gceist, lena chaidreamh i gcontae na Gaillimhe leis na daoine ba mhó tuigbheáil ar chúrsaí drámaíochta in Éirinn an ama sin. Ní heol dom go raibh a leithéid de chuidiú le fáil ag aon duine eile de dhrámadóirí luatha na Gaeilge.

Níorbh é de hÍde an t-aon drámadóir Gaeilge amháin a raibh baint aige le Gaillimh ag tús na haoise seo caite ach, is dóigh liom, caithfear an chreidiúint a thabhairt dó féin agus dá leathbhádóir Lady Gregory[50] as daoine eile as Gaillimh a spreagadh agus b'fhéidir a threorú i dtreo na drámaíochta.[51] Is iad na drámadóirí Gaillmheacha is luaithe a gcuimhnítear orthu ag tús na haoise seo caite: Séamas Ó Beirn,[52] Lorcán Ó Tuathail[53] agus Tomás Mac Amhalghaidh.[54]

Bhí daoine eile ann, áfach, a scríobh drámaí Gaeilge ansin go luath san aois seo caite agus nach bhfuil iomrá ar bith orthu, mar atá, Domhnall Ó Duibhne,[55] Tomás Ó

Colmáin,[56] Séamas Ó Maoildhia,[57] Mícheál Breathnach,[58] Tomás Breathnach,[59] Seosamh Ó Néill[60] srl.[61] Is deacair a chreidbheáil gur as a stuaim féin a thosaigh na daoine seo uilig ag saothrú na drámaíochta Gaeilge san áit agus san am chéanna sin.[62] Mar shampla, is léir go raibh seanaithne ag Lady Gregory ar bheirt mhúinteoirí ag casadh an chéid seo caite i gceantar an Spidéil:

> *Describing a visit to Spiddal, she told him ... she had regretted her ignorance of Irish when she had to enlist the help of two Irish-speaking schoolmasters to obtain stories for him.*[63]

Seans maith go raibh sí ag tagairt ansin do Dhomhnall Ó Duibhne[64] mar dhuine den bheirt sin. Is léir tionchar Lady Gregory ar Dhomhnall Ó Duibhne ar bhealach eile fosta óir chuir sé (mar atá, Daniel Deeney) leabhar amach darbh ainm *Peasant Lore from Gaelic Ireland* (London: David Nutt, 1900) a ndearna W.B. Yeats léirmheas air in *The Speaker*.[65]

Tá an comhoibriú, an cuidiú agus an spreagadh a fuair de hÍde ó Lady Gregory agus a comhluadar liteartha cíortha go maith ag lucht taighde cheana. Murach sin, drochsheans go mbeadh oiread drámaí Gaeilge maíte ar de hÍde agus atá.[66] Ach cén ceangal atá ag na drámadóirí Gaillmheacha Gaeilge eile le dreibhlín liteartha sin an Bhéarla i nGaillimh? Is leor nod don eolach. Tá an méid seo a leanas scríofa ag Lady Gregory in alt léi '*'The Whirligig of Time and the Irish Language*':[67]

> *I have lately been seeing some Irish plays acted, and translating others, and a few days ago one was sent me in manuscript from a workhouse school.*

Shamhlóinn sa chás atá luaite aici ansin gur Lorcán Ó Tuathail[68] a bhí i gceist aici, fear, mar atá a fhios againn óna bhfuil ráite cheana sa leabhar seo, a bhfuil drámaí Gaeilge scríofa aige agus a bhí ag an am sin ina mhúinteoir sa '*workhouse*.' Ní heol dúinn cad a tharla don lámhscríbhinn sin ó Theach na mBocht! Is cinnte, áfach, an saothrú ar fad a bhí ar siúl ar chúrsaí drámaíochta agus an caidreamh a bhí idir dream an Bhéarla agus dream na Gaeilge i gcomharsanacht na Gaillimhe ar leibhéil áirithe agus ar ócáidí áirithe, gur spreag sé an dá dhream ar bhealaí éagsúla ó thaobh na drámaíochta de. Tá tábhacht fosta ag baint le dátaí cumtha na ndrámaí Béarla agus Gaeilge seo agus go raibh feiseanna á reáchtáil thart orthu a thug deis na drámaí a stáitsiú.

Mar Mhúinteoir Taistil i gCo. Mhuineacháin

Is cosúil gur fhág Lorcán a phost múinteoireachta i nGaillimh agus gur thosaigh sé mar mhúinteoir taistil faoi scáth Chonradh na Gaeilge sa bhliain 1906. Bhí scéim le haghaidh theagasc na Gaeilge curtha ar siúl i Muineachán Thuaidh agus ceapadh Lorcán i gceannas na scéime sa bhliain 1906.[69]

> *A teaching scheme for the northern half of the county (Monaghan) has just been perfected, and at a meeting held at Muineachán on Friday evening last, Labhras Ó Tuathail, of Gaillimh... was selected to fill the post. He will commence work in about a fortnight.*[70]

Chuaigh sé ó thuaidh ar an 17 Samhain agus chaith beagnach bliain sa phost. Cuireadh ranganna ar siúl i naoi n-ionad. Bunaíodh craobh i gCluain Eois chomh maith le rang i gcomhair múinteoirí; dúradh ag an am gurbh é an chéad uair é a raibh obair eagraithe ar mhaithe leis an Ghaeilge ar siúl sa bhaile sin. Ní raibh aon mhí nár tuairiscíodh ranganna agus craobhacha a bheith ag dul i líonmhaire. Ní miste na cuntais seo a leanas ó nuachtáin logánta a thabhairt anseo le tuairim a thabhairt faoin chineál oibre a bhí ar siúl ag Lorcán i Muineachán.

> *Labhras Ua Tuathail GL teacher and Organiser for N. Monaghan – meeting in Monaghan fógartha ag Cumann na Múinteoirí Náisiúnta le hoideachas bunscoile a phlé.*[71]
>
> *A meeting of the North Monaghan Coisde Ceanntair of the Gaelic League was held in the Catholic Hall, Monaghan ... the following arrangements were made with regard to the work of the Travelling Teacher (Mr. L. O'Toole):*
> *Saturday: Teachers' class in Clones, from 10.15 a.m. to 12.15 p.m.;*

teachers' class in Smithboro from 12.45 p.m. to 2.45 p.m.;
Monaghan teachers' class, from 4.00 p.m. to 6.00 p.m.
Sunday teachers' class in the parishes of Donagh and Errigal Truagh.
Monday: Teaching during the day in several schools around Clones, and at night teaching the Clones Gaelic League class.
Tuesday: Teaching during the day in schools around Threemilehouse, and at night teaching Threemilehouse Gaelic League class.
Wednesday: Teaching during the day in schools around Aghabog and Latnamard, and at night teaching the local Gaelic class.
Thursday: Teaching during the day in schools around Smithboro and at night Smithboro class.
Friday: teaching during the day in schools around Scotstown, and a teachers' class and the Scotstown Gaelic class on Friday night.
Big Gaelic League night in Clones addressed at length by Pearse et al.[72]
Gaelic classes were instructed in Largy School, Clones, on Friday and Monday nights by Mr. Lorcan O'Toole, Irish Teacher for North Monaghan.[73]

Seo a leanas an chéad tuairisc a chuir Lorcán Ó Tuathail isteach maidir lena chuid oibre i gCo. Mhuineacháin mar a tuairiscíodh ar an *Anglo-Celt* (1/12/1906, 11).

The following report was submitted by the travelling teacher (Mr. L. O'Toole):
The number of schools which I have visited since I took up duty on November 5th was 19. The total number of visits which I have paid to these schools was 29; and I have given lessons of an hour's duration in practically the whole of them. In all the schools which I have visited I found unanimous desires among the children (one boy alone excepted) to learn the language of their country. This pleasing feature is due in no small degree to the splendid example set them by both priests and teachers of the various districts. Evening classes for adults are conducted in accordance with the arrangements made by your Committee. The attendance, on the whole, has been remarkably good, and the enthusiasm displayed by the students, one and all, leads one to hope that they will continue to operate in the revival of the Gaelic tongue in North Monaghan. The large increase in the evening class at Clones has necessitated its division into two sections; one for beginners, another for those who have had a

previous knowledge of the language – the latter being chiefly pupils and ex-pupils of the Convent School. A similar division must be made at Smithboro and Scotstown if the attendance at the opening classes in these centres is maintained. The classes at Aghabog and Threemilehouse are too large to be taught effectually in one division. The teachers' class at Ballyocean on Sundays has been discontinued, and instead I held two classes – one at Carrickruadh and another at Corracrin – on Sunday last by arrangement with the local committee. Carrickruadh would seem to be a good centre for a teachers' class, but Corracrin would not. The number present at the former centre was nine, and this, I believe, could be increased. The number of teachers who attended the Corracrin class was 4 – all daily teachers, none of whom, it appears, would find it convenient to go to any other centre on Sunday other than Corracrin or Ballyocean. Three of these teachers are working energetically for a teacher's certificate to teach Irish, and so it would be well to make some arrangement by which they could conveniently come to a teachers' class. If they could attend the Monaghan class on Saturdays, all would be well and then another teachers' class could be established elsewhere in the parish of Donagh, followed by a class for adults in the evening. A class for adults is already being held at Corracrin by Mr. O'Daly, as you are already aware. I would like, with the approval of your committee, to pay an occasional visit to those schools in which singing is taught, and not at present included in the nine different centres over which I have charge, for the purpose of having the children taught Irish songs, instead of English songs, which they sing at present. In several schools I have begun to teach these already.

Aithníodh láithreach go raibh an t-ualach oibre seo róthrom d'aon duine amháin: '*The advisability of employing another teacher to assist the travelling teacher, who had too much work to do already, was considered.*'

Anuas ar theagasc na Gaeilge, bhí amhránaíocht agus damhsaí mar chúram air fosta. *It was announced that Mr. O'Toole would give instruction in Irish jig dancing on class evenings in future.*[74]

Ní hiontas ar bith agus an obair agus an taisteal sin ba dhual don mhúinteoir taistil le déanamh aige, gur buaileadh tinn é anois is arís:

The Múinteoir Taistil, Lorcán Ua Tuathail, was unable to attend on Wednesday as he is suffering from a severe cold.[75]

Bhí tuairiscí anois is arís ar *An Claidheamh Soluis* faoi obair Lorcáin i Muineachán.[76]

Foilsíodh tuairiscí ó Lorcán féin ar an nuachtán logánta cúpla babhta ina dhiaidh sin fosta m.sh. *'Travelling Teacher's Report', The Anglo-Celt* (2/2/1907, 4) agus *The Anglo-Celt* (2/3/1907, 7).[77] As sin amach faighimid cuntais thall is abhus i nuachtáin éagsúla ar an obair mhór a bhí ar siúl aige agus é ag obair i Muineachán.

Mar Mhúinteoir Taistil i mBaile Átha Cliath

Fógraíodh ar *An Claidheamh Soluis* (14 Meán Fómhair 1907): *'Lorcán Ó Tuathail – who, by the way, has just brought out an English version of his popular* An Deoraidhe *– is coming as múinteoir taistil to Cuala. His work in North Muineachán will be taken up by two múinteoirí – it has grown too big for one'.*[78] Thug sé a aghaidh ar Bhaile Átha Cliath agus chrom ar a chuid oibre láithreach.

Irish in Dublin Schools

At the committee meeting of the Fr. Anderson Branch of the Gaelic League, held on Tuesday night at the rooms, 4 Lr. Sandwith St., Seorse O Diolan (leas-uachtaran) presiding, an runaire (Lorcan Ua Tuathail) stated that in compliance with the circular recently issued by the Education Committee of the Gaelic League re extending the teaching of Irish in the schools, he had written to the managers of the various schools in the parish asking that the Irish language be placed on the programme and timetable of all the schools, and that Irish history should be taught in the schools also, and he had received the following favourable reply from the Rev. Father Brady, Adm., Westland Row:

St. Andrew's, Westland Row, July 20:

'My dear Mr. O'Toole – your communication regarding our schools will have my best attention. I need not tell you that I shall be only too glad to forward the language movement by every means in my power, both in and out of our schools. Wishing you every success and blessing in your efforts to forward the interests of the noble cause, and again assuring you that nothing will be left undone by me

as far as parochial influence goes. I remain, dear Mr. O'Toole, very faithfully yours,

James Brady, Adm.'

An Runaire was directed to convey to Father Brady the best thanks of the committee for his patriotic action in the matter.[79]

Connradh na Gaedhilge

Coiste Comhairle Uí Chualainn

A meeting of the above Committee was held in the National Schools, Ballybrack, on Wednesday, the 4th inst., at 8.30 o'clock. Seaghan O'Reagain, President, in the chair. There were also present : Seoisimh Mac Tullecain (Ballybrack), Tomas O'Lalor (Dalkey), Seaghan O'Byrne (Dunleary), and Enri M.J. O'Hanluain, secretary; Lorcan Ua Tuathail, Muinteoir Taisteal was also in attendance.

A letter was read from the Coiste Ceanntair Baile Atha-Cliath informing the Coiste of a grant-in-aid, which generous treatment was greatly appreciated by the Committee as it enabled them to look forward to a year's hard work without misgiving. The appointment of Mr. Lorcan O'Tuathail, of Galway, as travelling teacher to the Committee, was ratified, and the work he would have to do in the schools in South Dublin was gone into in detail. It was decided to start him at once, and it is to be earnestly hoped that when the Muinteoir goes round he will be given every facility by both managers and teachers, and thus enabled to teach Irish in a thorough-going manner in the schools of the district. No make-believe work will do. The mockery and dishonesty of teaching Irish for half an hour a week and such periods as that ought to be dropped, as no good can accrue to either teachers or children from such a ridiculous way of humbugging Irish Irelanders and the public.

The teacher will start working in the branches from the 1st October next, when they will reopen, his programme there being nearly settled also.[80]

In Cuala

The appointment of Lorcán Ó Tuathail of Galway as Travelling Teacher to the Committee was ratified, and the work he will have to do in the schools in South Dublin was gone into in detail. It was decided to start him at once in the Ballybrack Boys' School, Loughlinstown, Tillystown and Cornelstown Girls', being five schools in all.[81]

Conradh na Gaedhilge

Coiste Comhairle Ui Cualainn

The usual meeting of the above was held in the National Schools, Seancill, on Sunday, the 29th ult. Seaghan O'Reagain (Uactaran) in the chair, and there were present: – Seosaimh MacTuileain (Craobh Ballybrack), Seaghan O'Byrne (Dunlaoghaire Branch), Tomas O'Lalor (Dalkey Branch), Padraig O'Murchadha (Seancill Branch), Lorcan O'Tuathaill, Travelling Teacher, and Enri M.S. O'Hanluain, Hon. Sec., were also present.

Correspondence was read from the Coisde Gnotha asking for a detailed account of the status of Irish in the schools of the district. It was decided to compile the required information, with the assistance of the Branches, and send it on to the Coiste Gnotha through the Coiste Ceanntair Baile Atha Cliath. Secretaries of Branches are therefore requested to go round to the schools ('National' Board), both Catholic and non-Catholic, in their districts and note down the information on the tabulated forms that will be supplied by the Secretary. The following is a translation of the report of Lorcan O'Tuathail, the Muinteoir Taisdeal, supplied to the meeting.

Report of the Travelling Teacher

A Chairde

I enclose a tabulated list of information about the schools in which I have been teaching this last fortnight. I am very glad to report that the children have a great liking for their language, and put all their hearts into the work. As far as I can see they seem determined to forge ahead until they are able to read and (sic) and write it with facility.

It is only right to say that the teachers have given me great help in encouraging the children generally in their work, and to attend regularly. I unfortunately had not time to see many of the clergy. The one gentleman I met (Father Connell) is a genuine Irish-Irelander, and signs of Canon O'Hea's (the parish priest's) help have been found everywhere.

I am sorry to report that the attention is not given to Irish History which that very important subject deserves.

It is true that the teachers are required to have a 'History Reader' as well as a 'Literary Reader.' But I am very much afraid it is but a trick to deceive the people, for it has been noticed by many that when the Inspector comes round he merely inquires is there a 'History Reader' used, and then turns to the 'Literary Reader' for the examination, and so the rules of the Commissioners are kept in the letter, but, alas, not in the spirit. In fact, I am afraid that the

Inspector is not required to examine out of the 'History Reader' at all.

There is but one school in this parish (Ballybrack) in which Irish is not taught, viz., the Workhouse School (girls), and I would recommend the Coiste Comhairle to look after the matter.

Is mise le meas mor,

Lorcan O'Tuathail,

Dalkey, September 29, 1907.[82]

Coiste Chomhairle Chualann a d'fhostaigh é mar mhúinteoir taistil an babhta seo. Cúig scoil náisiúnta i ndeisceart Chontae Bhaile Átha Cliath a bhí i gceist: an Baile Breac, Baile Uí Lachtnáin, Tillystown (Seanchill) agus Cúirt an Choirnéil. Mhúineadh sé ar feadh dhá uair an chloig i ngach scoil díobh. Thosaigh sé freisin ag múineadh i gClochar na Trócaire i mBaile an Bhóthair.[83] Bhíothas ag caint ar an dara múinteoir a cheapadh[84] ach faoi Bhealtaine bhí craobh bunaithe aige i Ráth Fearnáin agus bhí sé le tosú ag teagasc i gClochar Ghlas Tuathail.

In Cuala

It is thought that the Brí Craobh will shortly be in a position to ally itself with Coiste Comhairle Cualann, a step which will enable the Coiste to reinforce Labhras Ó Tuathail by appointing an additional Múinteoir. Labhras' time is fully occupied with school and Craobh work.[85]

Luadh ainm Lorcáin go poiblí thart ar an am seo fosta faoi ábhar eile ar fad.

SOUTH DOCK Ward

To the Editor of the Freeman's Journal

Dublin, January 9th

Dear Sir,

In the report of the Proceedings of the County Dublin Board of the G.A.A. published in your issue of this day I find that that body has recommended the names of three members of their Association as candidates at the municipal elections on Wednesday next – viz. Mr. Daniel MacCarthy (Merchant's Quay), Mr. Denis D. Healy (Usher's Quay), and Mr. Michael O'Flanagan (Rotunda) – and I am surprised that the County Board has overlooked the name of Mr.

Thomas M. O'Beirne (South Dock Ward). Mr. O'Beirne was an active member of the G.A.A. in London some years ago, and since he came to reside in Dublin he has been connected with the Association, both as a member of the Sunday Football League and as an official of the Red Branch Knights G.F.C. I am sure the County Board has unintentionally omitted Mr. O'Beirne's name from their resolution: but, as there are a number of supporters of the G.A.A. resident in the South Dock Ward, I consider it my duty to correct any misapprehension which may exist in the matter. Thanking you in anticipation, do chara, Lorcan Ua Tuathail.[86]

Is cosúil gur aithíodh cumas Lorcáin mar scoláire Gaeilge agus mar mhúinteoir nó ceapadh é ina ollamh le Gaeilge i gcoláiste oiliúna Dhún Chéirí (*An Claidheamh Soluis,* 10 Deireadh Fómhair 1908, 10), mar chomharba, b'fhéidir, ar Thomás Ó Nualláin.[87]

A Travelling Teacher's Success

Mr. Lorcan O'Toole, who up to recently has acted as travelling teacher of Irish for the Cuala district of South Dublin, has been selected for the professorship of Irish in the Training College of Our Lady of Mercy, Carysfort Park, Blackrock. Mr. O'Toole is a native speaker of Irish, and has considerable experience in teaching both Irish and English, having been trained in St. Patrick's Training College, Drumcondra. He is also the author of a number of works in the Irish Language, including the well-known play 'An Deoraidhe' which has been acted with success in Dublin, London, and elsewhere.[88]

Ar an drochuair ní raibh sé i bhfad sa phost sin nuair a buaileadh tinn é agus fuair sé bás ar an 28 Eanáir, 1909 agus é dhá scór bliain d'aois. Bhain a bhás siar as lucht na Gaeilge, muintir na Gaillimhe ach go háirithe a raibh aithne mhaith aige orthu agus níor fhág siad fuíoll molta air.

Gaedheal maith eile ar lár! Go ndéanaidh Dia trócaire air. Is beag a cheapamar nuair a chonnacamar fá Nodlaig é go mbeadh Lorcán Ó Tuathail faoi'n bhfód indiu. Sgéal ná sguan níor chualamar go raibh sé tinn go bhfacamar fuagra a bháis sna páipéaraibh. Rugadh i Maigh Chuilinn é agus sí an Ghaedhilge an chéad teanga labhair sé riamh. Bhí sé ag dul ar aghaidh go maith sa saoghal. Rinneadh ollamh dhe i gColáiste Carisfort anuaraidh. Is mór an lear oibre ghníodh sé ar son na Gaedhilge i nGaillimh agus ní dhéanfamuid dearmad go deo ar an gcéad oidhche léirigheadh 'An Deóraidhe'. Tá brón mór ar a chuid chomh-Gaillimheacha fá'n a bhás. Solus na bhflaitheas dá anam.

Pádhraic Ó Domhnalláin[89]

Lorcán Ó Tuathail a D'Éag

Gaedheal eile ar lár againn. Lorcán Ó Tuathail 'sé do chuaidh ar shlighe na fírinne an bobhta seo. Bhí aithne mhaith agam féin ar Lorcán bocht, agus b'aithne ar naomh agam é. Fíor-Ghaedheal cneasta, fear fóghlumta i dteanga a thíre, duine gan gangaid, gan deoch-bhéas gan anachan do b'eadh é. I Mágh Chuilinn, i gCo. na Gaillimhe do rugadh é. I Mágh Chuilinn do cuireadh é. Fuair sé bás i nOisbidéal Máthara na Trócaire i mBaile Átha Cliath Dé Céadaoin seo chuaidh thart. Níl aon chall agam morán a rádh mar gheall ar a dheagh-thréithibh is a mhaitheasa. Tuigfidh Gaedhil Chonndae Mhuineacháin is Chatharach na Gaillimhe is choisde cheanntair Bhrí Cualainne gur togha na bhfear a bhí ann. Ní raibh sé ag éagcaoin acht cúpla lá, agus is beag an tsúil a bhí ag á n-a cháirdibh nuair a chualadar i dtaoibh a thinnis gurabh é an bás a bhí ar ndaoine bocht ag saothrughadh.

Grádh a chroidhe is méid a mheanman do thug sé do'n Gaedhilge is d'obair Chonnartha na Gaedhilge. Ní go leor cainnte a bhí as ariamh, acht is fada an lá é ag obair go fial is go fearamhail; agus is i ngan fhios do'n tsaoghal do rinne sé cion fir ar son na cúise do ghrádhuigh a chroidhe. Ba é Lorcán a sgríobh 'An Deoraidhe' agus deirtear nár buaileadh fós é ar chlisteacht mar úr-chluichthe.

Níor cuireadh a 'Lá an Chíosa' i gcló fós cé gur léirigheadh ar ardán nó dhó é. Níl dul síar uaidh nár thuig sé sprid is inntinn a chomharsan, agus nach raibh geann is meas aige ar na daoinibh 'n-ar rugadh is tóigeadh i n-a measg é, agus ní h-é amháin ar son an tsean-nádúir ba dual dá chroidhe féin, acht ar son na Gaedhealtachta is na béasa geanamhla ba léir dó a bheith fighte fuaidhte i n-a gcroidhthibh.

Solus na Flaitheasa ag t-anam, a Lorcáin.[90]

Lorcán Ó Tuathail

> Tá Gaedheal maith eile d'éis bháis .i. Lorcán Ó Tuathail, go ndéana Dia trócaire ar a anam. Bhuail slaghdán é tá scathamh ó shoin ann agus níor thug sé aon aire dhó féin. Rug an slaghdán greim ar na scamhógaibh air annsin agus fá dheireadh b'éigin an duine bocht a chur isteach san osbuidéal. Ní raibh sé i bhfad san osbuidéal gur cailleadh é. Bhí sé tamall 'na mhúinteóir taistil fá'n tuath. Tháinig sé go hÁth Cliath annsin & chaith sé tamall eile 'na mhúinteóir taistil i mBrí Cualann. I dtús an tseisiúin seo ceapadh mar oide Gaedhilge i gColáiste Carysford ar an gCarraig Dhuibhe (sic), agus anois thug an bás leis é i mbláth a óige & a mhaitheasa. Ba cruaidh croidheamhail & ba dílis dúthrachtach an buachaill é, go ndéana Dia grásta ar a anam. Is é sgríobh an dráma sin ar a dtugtar 'An Deoraidhe.' Tá sé ceathair nó cúig do bhliadhantaibh ó sgríobh sé 'An Deoraidhe.' Ní raibh sé 'na mhúinteoir taistil an am (sic) sin ná ní raibh an oiread d'eolus ar an saoghal aige agus bhí ó shoin, acht taisbeáineann an dráma go raibh an mianach ann. Dá bhfaghadh an fear bocht saoghal níl aon aimhreas agam nach ndéanfadh sé obair mhaith fós do'n teangaidh Ghaedhilge.
> Eoghan Ó Neachtain[91]

Ní raibh saol fada i ndán do Lorcán Ó Tuathail. Ba laoch eile de chuid luathstair na hAthbheochana é nach bhfuil mórán iomrá air inniu. Gaeilgeoir breá a bhí ann a fáisceadh as dúchas láidir, Gaelach; fear a bhí ann a tháinig faoi anáil na hAthbheochana agus a rinne a chion féin ar son na cúise céanna, mar mhúinteoir Gaeilge, mar mhúinteoir taistil agus mar dhrámadóir Gaeilge a chothaigh spiorad agus idé-eolaíocht na hAthbheochana bealach a chuid drámaíochta. Ní fios cén lorg a d'fhágfadh sé ar stair na Gaeilge dá ndeonófaí saol fada dó ag treabhadh ghort na Gaeilge fá shuaimhneas ina phost úr. Táimid faoi chomaoin mhór aige as ar éirigh leis a chur i gcrích sa saol gearr a chaith sé.

IN LOVING MEMORY
OF
JOHN O' TOOLE
DIED 4TH MARCH 1937
AGED 69 YEARS
HIS SON JERMIAH
DIED 7TH OCT. 1933 AGED 20 YEARS
HIS BROTHERS
LAWRENCE DIED 2TH JAN 1909
AGED 40 YEARS
FRANCIS DIED 5TH MAY 1898
AGED 26 YEARS
PAT DIED 9TH MARCH 1940
HIS WIFE BRIGID
DIED 15TH FEBRUARY 1950
AND THEIR DAUGHTER
ANGELA DIED 2ND MAY 1998
R.I.P.
ERECTED BY HIS WIFE & FAMILY

Nótaí

1 Níl aon chuimhne air i Maigh Cuilinn agus cailleadh cibé cáipéisí agus grianghraif a bhain le muintir Uí Thuathail i ndóiteán roinnt mhaith blianta ó shin.

2 Lorcán agus Labhrás a tugadh air i rith a shaoil. Agus muid ag cur síos air sa leabhar seo, tugaimid Lorcán air i gcónaí ar mhaithe le héascaíocht.

3 Dúradh in *An Claidheamh Soluis* (6 Feabhra 1909, 6) gur i Maigh Cuilinn, Co. na Gaillimhe, a rugadh é.

4 Baile fearainn cúpla míle ó shráidbhaile Mhaigh Cuilinn.

5 Baisteadh é ar 16 Eanáir, 1870 de réir liosta na mbaistí i Leabharlann Náisiúnta na hÉireann.

6 Ainm.ie

7 *An Claidheamh Soluis* (29/4/1899, 109). *'Branches of the Gaelic League were formed last month at... Moycullen.' An Claidheamh Soluis* (18/3/1899, 12).

8 *An Claidheamh Soluis* (27/1/1900, 725).

9 Ainm.ie agus Aingeal Ní Chualáin, *Tomás Bairéad: Rogha Scéalta* (Cló Iar-Chonnacht, 2010).

10 Féach: ainm.ie.

11 Chláraigh Ciarán Ó Concheanainn amhráin Ghaeilge na barúntachta ina leabhar *Clár Amhrán Mhaigh Cuilinn* (Comhairle Bhéaloideas Éireann, 2011) agus chuir Pádraic Breathnach cnuasach béaloidis ón cheantar i gcló ina leabhar *Maigh Cuilinn: a Táisc agus a Tuairisc* (Cló Chonamara, 1986). Is fiú an leabhar le Treasa Mhic Mhathúna, *Craobh Mhaigh Cuilinn de Chonradh na Gaeilge* (1994) a lua anseo freisin.

12 Foilsíodh alt *'The National Teachers and Primary Education in Ireland'* le John R.M. Curtin faoi mhúinteoirí Thithe na mBocht in *The Galway Observer* (30/5/1896, 3).

13 *Galway Observer* (30/5/1896, 2). Cláraíodh Lorcán mar bhall de Chumann na Múinteoirí Náisiúnta in 1895. *The National Teacher* (22/11/1895, 570). Tá mé buíoch de Dhara Ó Cualáin as an tagairt seo.

14 Sa Daonáireamh ní thugtaí ach túslitreacha ainmneacha na ndaoine i dTeach na mBocht ach bhí A.H. (10), M.B. (10) agus J.C. (10) i measc na leanaí ann. Bhí Gaeilge acu go léir agus gach seans gurbh iad sin Art Ó hInsí, Máirtín de Búrca agus Seán Ó Cléirigh a bhuaigh duaiseanna úd an Chliabhraigh do na daltaí ab fhearr Gaeilge sna bunscoileanna. (Baineadh an t-eolas seo as ainm.ie).

15 Bhí cáil ar Euseby Digby Cleaver mar réamhchonraitheoir a chaith go hiontach fial le hAthbheochan na Gaeilge i rith a shaoil. Bhronnadh sé duaiseanna chun teagasc na teanga a spreagadh i scoileanna na Gaeltachta, mar shampla. Tá cuntas air le fáil in ainm.ie.

16 *An Claidheamh Soluis* (1 Feabhra, 1902, 785).

17 Léiríodh é, mar shampla, ag Feis Chonnacht sa bhliain 1903. B'fhéidir gurbh é an dráma seo a leanas atá i gceist ag Yeats sa phíosa seo a leanas: "*...of all the performances of Gaelic plays in the country during the year I have seen but one – Dr. Hyde's play, Cleamhnas, at Galway Feis. I got there a day late for a play by the Master of the Galway Workhouse, but heard that it was well played, and that his dialogue was as good as his construction was bad...'* *Samhain* (September 1903) 3. Tá mé buíoch de Dhara Ó Cualáin (OÉ, Gaillimh) as an tagairt seo.

18 Seo a leanas an réamhrá a cuireadh leis an chuntas seo.
Ah, but the olden spirit glints from that wine-dark eye,
Mark you those lips, still rose red and firm set as of yore,
Let but her Eire's battle-challenge pierce the sky
She'll leap to life once more.
The Gaelic League has now been ten years in existence and I may safely say that already it has far exceeded in extent and influence the hope of its founders. Ireland is phenomenal for the waxing and waning of leagues; but the Gaelic League must be considered apart. Its growth has been slow and healthy and its ideal is broad and national. It has brought a new spirit into the people, a manly, independent spirit, which was badly needed, and which promises to grow apace and be a main factor in moulding the future of the country. For many years now we have been gradually renouncing our independence, especially our independence of thought. We receive our ideas and ideals in literature and art second-hand from London and elsewhere, just as ladies do the 'fashions.' And just as the scraps of fashion that reach a country town here are not like the style of the lords and ladies, but rather like that of the factory girl and the Cockney and, moreover, reach us years behindhand. So our intellectual ideals are not the newest or the best, but rather the cast-off shoddy of other peoples. The Gaelic League says we must change all that. We must wake up. We must make ideas, ideals and fashions for ourselves. Away with shoddy, whether mental, material or intellectual.

19 *The Galway Observer* (29/8/1903). Bhí an fear seo ó Sylane i gCo. na Gaillimhe ina dhochtúir leighis agus scríobh sé dráma i gcomhar le Lorcán Ó Tuathail. Bhí deartháir aige, an Dr.

Micheál Breathnach, a ndúradh faoi: '*He has also collaborated with his brother, Dr. T. Walsh, in the writing of some clever Irish plays. The Galway Express* (16/11/1907, 3).

Chuir an Piarsach síos ar an dráma seo mar '*a blending of the tragedy and comedy of the land war*' nuair a léiríodh é ag Feis Chonnacht sa bhliain 1903. Féach, 'Feis Chonnacht,' *An Claidheamh Soluis* (29/8/1903).

Tugann Philip O'Leary an tuairisc seo a leanas air in *The Prose Literature of the Gaelic Revival 1881–1921: Ideology and Innovation* (The Pennsylvania State Universiy Press, 1994) 196–7.

Landlord tyranny and the specter of eviction are the subject of three important early Gaelic plays, Labhras Ua Tuathail's ***Lá an Chíosa*** *(Rent day) (1903), Tomás Ó Ceallaigh's* ***Ar Thaoibh an Locha*** *(Beside the Lake) (1908), and Hyde's* ***Maistín an Bhéarla*** *(The Bully of the English language). All three works dramatize the anguish of a farmer threatened with the loss of his holding, and the first two resolve the crisis with a facile and unconvincing* ***deus ex machina*** *climax. In the former the greedy landlord Manders seems to undergo an instantaneous conversion to human decency when his wife points out that he hasn't been a very nice person. At play's end, he sacks his unscrupulous agent and vows to do his utmost to keep his tenants safe, secure and at home in Ireland by allowing them to buy out their holdings at bargain rates.*

Léiríodh an dráma seo anois agus arís i rith na mblianta sin ach cuimhnítear go mbeadh deacracht ann an dráma a léiriú mura mbeadh fáil air i bhfoirm leabhair. Fógraíodh ar an *Western People* (13/2/1904, 8): '*the pupils of Treen (An Trian, Tuar Mhic Éadaigh, Co. Mhaigh Eo) played 'Lá an Chíosa' before a very crowded house.*' Fógraíodh an bhliain dár gcionn ar an *Western People* (18/2/1905, 5): '*the Treen Club acted it in Tourmakeady.*' Is fiú a lua anseo freisin gur ardán iontach maith a bhí i bhFeis Chonnacht chun drámaí a spreagadh agus a léiriú. Féach, fosta, 'The Connacht Feis' in *An Claidheamh Soluis* (27/8/1904, 7).

Maidir le haighneas talmhaíochta i gContae na Gaillimhe ag deireadh an naoú haois déag, féach, Philip Bull, 'The Formation of the United Irish League 1898–1900: the Dynamics of Irish Agrarian Agitation' in *Irish Historical Studies* Vol. XXXIII (2002–3) 404–23 agus Conal Thomas, *The United Irish League and Land Reform in North Galway 1898–1912* (Annaghdown Heritage Society, 1999).

Féach, fosta, ar a bhfuil le rá faoin tréimhse seo i stair na hÉireann ag F.S.L. Lyons in *Ireland Since the Famine* (Fontana Press, eag. 1973) 216–20.

20 *An tsrothan* sa téacs.

21 Alt ag Lurcan Ua T. *(= Lorcán Ó Tuathail, drámadóir)* ar an *Galway Observer* (15/8/1903, 3).

22 *The Galway Observer* (22/8/1903, 4).

23 *The Galway Observer* (29/8/1903, 2).

24 Tá amhráin Choilm le fáil in Gearóid Denvir, *Amhráin Choilm de Bhailís* (CIC, 1996) agus cuntas ar a chuid filíochta ina alt 'Colm de Bhailís: File na nOileán' in *Oidhreacht na nOileán, Léachtaí Cholm Cille* XXII (1992) 136–63. Ní luaitear an comhfhreagras seo i gceachtar acu sin.

25 *The Galway Observer* (29/8/1903, 2).

26 Bhí an-tábhacht ag baint le feiseanna ar fud na tíre mar ardán do dhrámaí scríofa ag drámadóirí logánta.

27 Ghlac Pádraic Ó Conaire páirt i roinnt drámaí agus é thall i Londain ach ní luann an tSiúr Eibhlín Ní Chionnaith an ceann seo ina leabhar *Pádraic Ó Conaire: Scéal a Bheatha* (Cló Iar-Chonnachta, 1995) 105–6.

28 *Galway Express* (5/12/1903, 1).

ANOTHER IRISH DRAMA

A very pleasing drama was that of The Miser's Matchmaking, collaborated by Mr. E. L. O'Toole, schoolteacher at the workhouse, and Dr. T. Walsh, medical officer, Oranmore, and of which the following is a synopsis: 'A farmer returns from a fair well pleased with his day's work. His wife abuses him with being so late. He orders the daughter to tidy up the place as he expects strangers for matchmaking. The daughter declares that she will marry none but her lover, whose only fault appears to be that he is poor. The father pleads and finally insists that she must marry his selection who, as described by a neighbour who comes in, is a miserly, deformed creature. The miser comes in due accompanied by a friend, and after some hard bargaining the match is settled, but as this miser is not to be trusted, he is told to go for the money. During his absence the daughter's lover comes, accompanied by his uncle lately returned from America. This uncle offers to pay up all monies due by the father if he gives his daughter to the nephew. The father agrees as he has no liking for the miser and accepted him only to stave off pressing creditors. When the miser returns he asks 'Will she marry me now?' and is greatly surprised when told she will not. He then abuses all around him, especially the lover and the returned Yank, creating roars of laughter by telling the audience how the Yank 'made his money,' namely on the instalment 'system' in America. The Galway Express (25/8/1906, 5).

29 *IRISH PLAY BY A TUAM MAN*
We are glad to see that an Irish play has been brought out by a Tuam man. The play is called **Cleamhnas Crustóir** *and the author is Dr. Thomas Walsh, second son of the late Michael Walsh, N.T. of Sylane. Dr. Walsh is well-known in Gaelic circles, being one of the joint secs. of the Connaught Féis. He has had a distinguished career so far, and has taken his share of the literary spoils of the three Kingdoms. We understand he took the £50 prize for three years at Owen's College, Manchester, and graduated at the University of Edinburgh in 1901. His play has met with great success in London, the leading part, Eadmon Crustoir, being well acted by Mr. Thomas Grehan, of Salthill, Galway. The Tuam Herald* (5/12/1903, 4).

30 *The Tuam Herald* (2/9/1905, 4).

31 2 Aibreán 1904, 7.

32 Mar shampla, ag Feis Chonnacht (*An Claidheamh Soluis,* 27 Lúnasa 1904); ag Oireachtas 1905; i gCarna (*Ibid.,* 20 Eanáir 1906); léiriú Scoil Haverstock Hill i mí Bealtaine 1906 (*Conradh na Gaeilge i Londain* 1894–1917, 1989 le Donncha Ó Súilleabháin); ag Feis Chonnacht sa Spidéal (*An Claidheamh Soluis,* 3 Meán Fómhair 1910); léiriú Chraobh an Spidéil ag Oireachtas 1913 (*Scéal an Oireachtais 1897–1924,* 1984 le Donncha Ó Súilleabháin).

33 **The Exile** *by Lorcan O'Toole (Dublin: M.H. Gill and Son Ltd., 6d). As a Gaelic playwright, Mr. O'Toole is fast coming to the front. He is the author of 'The Rent Day,' 'Pious Daniel' and other dramas in Gaelic including 'An Deoraidhe' which he has now given us in an English dress under the above title. The play claims to be a 'faithful portrayal of the craze for emigration' in Ireland, and in its original form became very popular in Gaelic circles. It is certain to be a great success in its present form. The play has been very neatly printed at the Democrat Offices, Monaghan. The Galway Express* (24/8/1907, 5).

34 Bhí scéal na himirce chomh dona sin i ndiaidh an Ghorta Mhóir gur cuireadh eagraíocht ar bun i Meiriceá darbh ainm '*The Mission of Our Lady of the Rosary for the Protection of Irish Immigrant Girls*' i mí Dheireadh Fómhair 1883. Tá cuntas cuimsitheach foilsithe ag Maureen Murphy ar an eagraíocht sin in *irishamerica.com/2010/01/the-mission-girls/ updated March 2, 2012.*
Féach, fosta, a leithéid seo a leanas:
EMIGRATION
Important Appeal to the Irish in America

The greatest danger threatening Ireland today is the danger of the extinction of the Irish race within her own shores. For now nearly sixty years the flow of emigration has gone on continuously till the population of the country is reduced to one half what it was before the Famine. In the short space of the last twenty years ... no less than 910,000 men and women emigrated from Ireland to the United States alone. Of these 750,000, or 83 per cent., were in the prime of life, between the ages of 15 and 35 ... The loss of her young population to one country alone in the last twenty years was fully one half of the present adult population in the prime of life.

This enormous withdrawal of the most vigorous portion of the nation has had its natural results. The native population is steadily falling; the marriage rate and birth rate are the lowest of any civilised country; lunacy is increasing to an alarming degree; and the scarcity of labour is felt in many branches of agriculture... there is a steady, silent influx of foreigners who are rapidly constituting themselves the dominant commercial and industrial interest ... If this double process of emigration and 'plantation' be allowed to continue it is obvious that the native Irish will soon be entirely supplanted in their own land by people of other races ...

We appeal to the Irish-American and Catholic Press to educate public opinion on this vital question; we appeal to the Irish-American Bishops and Clergy to ask their people not to assist emigration from Ireland; and finally we appeal to the Irish organisations and societies in America to throw their United strength into the effort to hold Ireland as the cradleland of the race.

Signed:

Michael Cardinal Logue, Archbishop of Armagh, President of the Anti-Emigration Society,Thomas Fennelly, Archbishop of Cashel, John Healy, Archbishop of Tuam, R.A. Sheehan, Bishop of Waterford and Lismore, Vice-President of the Anti-Emigration Society, Joseph Hutchinson, Lord Mayor of Dublin, Douglas Hyde, President of the Gaelic League etc. The Ulster Herald (26/3/1904, 3).

Féach, fosta: *Our leading member of Parliament, Mr. John Redmond, in speaking in Killarney in October, 1903...(said): 'Many of the poor Irish (in America) scarcely lead the lives of human beings at all; they have no happiness, no health, no home life, and too often... no religion.' The Ulster Herald* (30/4/1904,7). Bhí eagarfhocail sna nuachtáin ag cáineadh na himirce agus filí agus scríbhneoirí ag scríobh ó chuile chearn den tír agus thar lear faoin cheist freisin.

35 *Freeman's Journal* (2/2/1904, 2). Féach, fosta, *The Evils of Emigration* by Richard Kelly (CTS pamphlet) 1902.

36 *The Galway Express* (27/8/1904, 3).

37 *AN DEORAIDHE*

The **Deoraidhe** *the coming of which has been for some time past announced in our columns has appeared in a neat little addition from the press of the Clóchumann with a vocabulary which facilitates the reading of it for learners of Irish ... In the short preface in which An Craoibhín recommends this work of Mr. O'Toole to the public he suggests that it be taken up as a reading book in schools and this is a suggestion which we would endorse for thoroughly idiomatic Irish, pure as nature placed it on the lips of Connaughtmen, for Irish of the real 'blas' it can hardly be surpassed. If Irish children are to be taught Irish they must be taught it in the form nature taught it to their fathers without any of the artificiality which is only too liable to be attached to it by some teachers and books of today. This artificiality is happily what is entirely wanting in* **An Deoraidhe**, *the most distinctive mark of which from beginning to end in its characters as its language is naturalness. The play itself – or as we would rather term it – the story is well worthy of the author of* **Lá an Chíosa**. *We do not say the piece shows great intricacy of plot, for that is not to be expected in so small a compass, but we do say that with the opportunities of space at his disposal, Mr. O'Toole has evolved a dramatic situation full of interest for Irishmen and Irishwomen and has forcibly laid before them the lesson that they must learn, the lesson of anti-emigration. On the stage or in the schoolroom the work will have its effect. It will give Irish children a thorough acquaintance with the Irish language, and it will amuse, and above all it will instruct the spectators who are fortunate enough to see it played. The fact that after its production on the first night of the Connaught Feis it had to be repeated on the second night by special request, is one which tells more in its favour than anything else.*

(*An Deoraidhe,* a propagandist play by E.L. O'Toole, price 6d net.) *The Connaught Champion* (13/5/1905, 2).

38 *The Leader* (12/11/1904, 180–1).

39 Tá cuntas cuimsitheach ag Máirín Ní Mhuiríosa ar Cleaver in *Réamhchonraitheoirí* (Clódhanna Teoranta, 1968) 58–68. Féach, fosta, ar ainm.ie agus http://dib.cambridge.org/ .

40 *An Claidheamh Soluis* (12/8/1905). Duilleachán an Oireachtais, 2, 4.

41 *Freeman's Journal* (23/2/1906, 14).

42 Gan amhras, is ceart a rá murach cáil a bheith ar Ghaillimh ó thaobh na drámaíochta Gaeilge de roimhe sin, drochsheans go lonnófaí téatar Gaeilge ansin.

Maidir le stair na drámaíochta Gaeilge i nGaillimh, féach ar an alt tábhachtach le Philip O'Leary, '*What Would Willie Say? Lady Gregory and Popular Theatre in Irish*' in *The Journal of the Galway Archaeological and Historical Society* Vol. 63 (2011, 158–180). Tá mé faoi chomaoin mhór ag an alt cuimsitheach sin sa taighde seo.

43 Luaitear in Gareth W. & Janet Egleson Dunleavy, *Douglas Hyde: a Maker of Modern Ireland* (University of California Press, 1991) 204 gur chas de hÍde agus Lady Gregory ar a chéile sa bhliain 1897.

Tugtar faoi deara an iontráil seo a leanas i ndialann Lady Gregory don bhliain 1898:

1st Sept[ember] – To Galway Feis with W.B.Y. to support the Gaelic movement – very glad we went, for none of 'the classes' were there to support it unless priests can be so called –

Greaney, the young Spiddal schoolmaster gave a recitation with gr vigour – & as Deeney the other master was giving the next, W.B.Y. asked Greaney what they were all about & he said "Both poems are called 'Thoughts on Ireland' – my one tells how the Sassenach baffled us entirely, & the one he's giving tells how the Sassenach murdered us a while ago" – very characteristic "Thoughts on Ireland" – James Pethica (ed.), *Lady Gregory's Diaries 1892–1902* (Colin Smythe, 1996) 188.

44 Tá achoimre maith déanta ag F.S.L. Lyons ar an chomhluadar liteartha sin in *Ireland Since the Famine* (Fontana Press, eag. 1973) 236:

The very fact that Hyde, Yeats, Lady Gregory and Synge should all have found the idiom and the rhythm so accessible was in itself no accident. It was a remarkable feature of their movement – and perhaps a partial explanation … of its success – that they should all have had, as did also George Moore and Edward Martyn, a common root in the west of Ireland… They not only shared a common background of country life, they were in close physical communication with each other. It was precisely this intimacy, this possibility of discussing and planning in private without the distraction of public meetings and committees, which allowed the new movement to develop so fast and which also, it must be said, gave it from the outset a distinctly autocratic character.

45 Gareth W. & Janet Egleson Dunleavy, *Selected Plays of Douglas Hyde* (Colin Smythe, 1991) 14. I gcuntas eile ag Gareth W. & Janet Egleson Dunleavy, *Douglas Hyde: a Maker of Modern Ireland* (University of California Press, 1991) 206, tá an cuntas seo a leanas: *In late December 1898, at Lady Gregory's invitation, Hyde*

and Norma Borthwick (who was then tutoring Lady Gregory in Irish and giving classes to local people in Lady Gregory's Coole Park gatehouse every afternoon) presented an Irish-language Punch-and-Judy show at a Christmas party for workhouse children. Hyde triumphed in scenes in which he scolded the baby in Irish… Deirtear san áit chéanna go raibh Lady Gregory i láthair nuair a thug de hÍde óráid ag bunú Chaobh Chill Tartan de Chonradh na Gaeilge ag tús na bliana dár gcionn.

46 Gareth W. & Janet Egleson Dunleavy, *Selected Plays of Douglas Hyde* (Colin Smythe, 1991) 15.

47 Dominic Daly, *The Young Douglas Hyde* (1974) 135.
Tá an cuntas seo a leanas ag Lady Gregory ar stair scríofa an dráma seo: '*[27th August] Hyde… began his 'Twisting of the Rope' and got on splendidly … 'Twisting of the Rop' splendid … [3 September] Hyde … has begun a new play on matchmaking.*' Luaite in James Pethica (ed.), *Lady Gregory's Diaries 1892–1902* (Colin Smythe, 1996) 278. Níos faide ar aghaidh deirtear: '*George Moore … likes 'Twisting of the Rope' and has made some small alterations to it.*' (op. cit. 279).

48 Gareth W. & Janet Egleson Dunleavy, *Selected Plays of Douglas Hyde* (Colin Smythe, 1991) 13–27.

49 Pethica, 312. Cuirtear leis an eolas seo i bhfonóta a thagraíonn don ráiteas sin: '*AG subsequently translated Hyde's plays 'The Lost Saint' and 'The Nativity' and included them in Poets and Dreamers. The 'Fearful Dream' was probably an early title for Hyde's play 'Pléusgadh na Bulgóide', based on an idea by AG, which he completed at Coole in August in 1902, and which she likewise translated (as 'The Bursting of the Bubble') and published in New Ireland Review, May 1903.*'

50 Ní raibh chuile dhuine den bharúil gur chara mór leis na Gaeil í Lady Gregory, rud a thugann E. Ó h-Éanacháin le fios ina alt 'Bail' Uí Lí' ar *Gearrbhaile* Iml. XXVI (1954) 25, 32. Níor aontaigh P.E. Mac Fhinn leis, áfach, in *Ar Aghaidh* (Aibreán, 1955) 1. (Tá mé buíoch de Mhicheál Ó Catháin as an eolas seo).

51 *THE FIRST GAELIC PLAYS*
Professor Liam Ó Briain
Sufficient credit has never been given, in my opinion, to Yeats and Lady Gregory, by the language movement. When they started their dramatic movement, they clearly wanted it to be bilingual and it was not their fault if it didn't develop in both languages pari passu. I think it was thanks to them that Dr. Hyde began to write plays. The Leader (14/3/1942, 157).

52 Féach, Diarmuid Breathnach agus Máire Ní Mhurchú, *1882–1982 Beathaisnéis a hAon* (An Clóchomhar, 1986) 48–9, agus Nollaig Mac Congáil, 'Fíoradh na Físe Gaelaí? Bunú Choláiste Thamhain 100 Bliain ó Shin: Stair Chorrach,' *Journal of the Galway Archaeological and Historical Society*, Vol. 62 (2010) 157–85. Ó thaobh na drámaíochta de, cuimhnítear air mar údar na ndrámaí *An Dochtúir* agus *Obair*.

53 Féach, Diarmuid Breathnach agus Máire Ní Mhurchú, *1882–1982 Beathaisnéis a Cúig* (An Clóchomhar, 1997) 258–9. Cuimhnítear air go náisiúnta mar údar na ndrámaí *An Deoraí* agus *Lá an Chíosa* ach go háirithe.

54 Níl aon chuntas faoi in *Beathaisnéis*. Ní fheicim aon chuntas faoi ag Mary Kavanagh in *Galway – Gaillimh: a Bibliography of the City and County* (Galway Co. Co., 2000).

55 Is fiú a lua anseo, b'fhéidir, gurbh é Jack B. Yeats a tharraing na léaráidí le haghaidh an leabhair *Páistidheacht* (1906) a chum Séamus Ó Beirn agus a chuir Domhnall Ó Duibhne in eagar agus tá Norma Borthwick faoi chomaoin aige fosta maidir lena sraith leabhrán *Ceachta Beaga Gaedhilge* a mhaisiú. Bhí comhoibriú agus caidreamh láidir idir na daoine seo ar fad breis is céad bliain ó shin.

56 Maidir le Tomás Ó Colmáin, tá cuntas faoi in Diarmuid Breathnach agus Máire Ní Nhurchú, *1882–1982 Beathaisnéis a Cúig* (An Clóchomhar Teo., 1997) 136–137.

57 Tá cuntas agam faoi in 'An Ghaeilge agus *The Connacht Tribune*' in Diarmuid Ó Cearbhaill (eag.), *Journal of the Galway Archaeological and Historical Society*, Vol. 61 (2009) 206–22.

58 Is é an Mícheál Breathnach atá i gceist anseo an duine seo a leanas.

Mr. Michael Walsh, B.A.

We are pleased to announce that the above-named young gentleman has won his honours B.A. degree at the Royal University. Mr. Walsh is a native of Sylane, and brother to Dr. Thomas Walsh, of Oranmore, and Mr. Richard Walsh, N.T., of Sylane, and nephew to Father Joyner, of Woodquay. The new B.A. has had a distinguished career as a scholar at Queen's College, Galway, where, after creditable achievements in the Intermediate, he received a junior scholarship together with a first University examination. In the following year he again won a literary scholarship and second University examination, in which he got an exhibition. In 1905–6 he got his third literary scholarship, and this year a senior exhibition in modern languages, and his B.A. degree. Mr. Walsh has been vice-chairman of the College Debating Society, and officially connected with the Catholic Students' Society since its inception. He has also collaborated with his brother, Dr. T. Walsh, in the writing of some clever Irish plays. We congratulate Mr. Walsh on his new-won honours, and wish him further successes in the literary world. (*The Galway Express*, 16/11/1907, 3).

59 Dochtúir leighis a raibh baint mhór aige le cúis na Gaeilge i nGaillimh. Scríobh sé dráma i gcomhar le Lorcán Ó Tuathail.

60 Féach, Diarmuid Breathnach agus Máire Ní Mhurchú, *1882–1982 Beathaisnéis a hAon* (An Clóchomhar, 1986) 92–3. Bhí sé ina mhac léinn san ollscoil i nGaillimh ó 1898 go dtí 1902. Bhain sé duais Oireachtais i roinn na ndrámaí gearra sa bhliain 1903 mar atá luaite ag Donncha Ó Súilleabháin in *Scéal an Oireachtais: 1897–1924* (An Clóchomhar Tta., 1984).

61 Níor cheart Pádraic Ó Conaire a lua sa chomhthéacs seo gí gur scríobh sé roinnt drámaí ó tharla go raibh sé ag baint faoi san am thall i Londain.

62 Is cinnte go raibh cúinsí iomadúla ann a chuidigh le cothú na drámaíochta Gaeilge go díreach nó go hindíreach i nGaillimh.
This year's Galway Feis should eclipse all its predecessors. Galway is, as we have said before, the natural capital of Gaelic Ireland. The county of Galway contains some places where Irish is cultivated under particularly favourable circumstances. The Arran Isles have been the place of pilgrimage of would-be Gaedhilgeoridhe for many years now, and an Inis Meadhoin man is now the chief organiser of the movement. At Spiddal the language enjoys the influential favour of the Morrises, which has certainly had a most beneficial effect. At Gort, Lady Gregory and Mr. Edward Martyn have been working energetically for the preservation of Irish. And besides, Galway actually contains the most out-and-out Irish spots of Ireland, where a man can walk for ten miles at a time without meeting a person who can answer the simplest question in English.
Fáinne an Lae (7/7/1900, 212).

63 Gareth W. & Janet Egleson Dunleavy, *Douglas Hyde: a Maker of Modern Ireland* (University of California Press, 1991) 206.

64 Tá cuntas cuimsitheach air ag Diarmuid Breathnach agus Máire Ní Mhurchú, *1882–1982 Beathaisnéis a Cúig* (An Clóchomhar, 1997) 111–3.

65 14/7/1900, 216.

66 *It is interesting to note that Mr. W.B. Yates (sic), the author of the 'Countess Kathleen,' was present at the Gaelic Feis, whilst Mr. Martyn, author of the 'Heather Field', who was unable to attend, sent some excellent suggestions in his letter of apology. Perhaps we are over*

sanguine, but we fancy that the interest of these two gentlemen in the Galway Feis... and the wish to produce something in the shape of a Gaelic play, which crops up every now and again in different parts of Connacht, may have their effect in making possible the production of a Gaelic play of some kind at the other side of the Shannon. Fáinne an Lae (30/9/1899, 101).

67 *The Tuam News and Western Advertiser* (5/12/1902, 3).

68 Féach, Diarmuid Breathnach agus Máire Ní Mhurchú, *1882–1982 Beathaisnéis a Cúig* (An Clóchomhar, 1997) 258–9.

69 *An Claidheamh Soluis* (3 Samhain 1906, 9).

Féach, fosta, Aindrias Ó Muimhneacháin, *Na Múinteoirí Taistil* (Conradh na Gaeilge, 1966), Donncha Ó Súilleabháin, *Na Timirí i Ré Tosaigh an Chonartha 1893–1927* (Conradh na Gaeilge, 1990) agus Colm Ó Cearúil, *Aspail ar Son na Gaeilge: Timirí Chonradh na Gaeilge 1899–1923* (Conradh na Gaeilge, 1995). Is fiú fosta breathnú ar an aiste seo a leanas ar shaol an mhúinteora taistil le léargas a fháil ar an chineál poist a bhí i gceist.

SAOL AN MHÚINTEORA TAISTIL

Tadhg Ó Rabhartaigh

Is beag dream ins an tír atá chomh gann leis na múinteoirí taistil Gaeilge. Tá siad scabtha i bhfad óna chéile ar fud mhóinte agus bhántaí Fáil. Is annamh a bhíos beirt acu níos deise ná fiche míle talaimh dá chéile agus is minic nach bhfaigheann siad a gcaint is a gcomhrá a dhéanamh le chéile ó cheann go ceann na bliana. Dá thairbhe sin de, ní bhíonn an t-áiméar ag an mhúinteoir taistil an cuidiú a fháil óna chómhúinteoirí a fhaigheas cineálacha eile múinteoirí. Bíonn fiche rud i gan fhios dó, barúil nó comhairle nó leideadh a bhéarfadh dóchas dó agus a chuideochadh go mór leis ina chuid oibre. Caitheann sé a dhóchas a chur ann féin agus a bheilt a theannadh air lena iomaire a threabhadh leis féin.

Duine dó féin é ins an phobal. Tá sé mar a bheadh an broc nó an ceann cait ann: nuair atá achan duine réidh lena lá oibre agus iad ag glacadh sómais chois tineadh le solas lampa, níl an múinteoir taistil gránna ach ag gabháil i gceann gnoithe. Oíche na seacht síon agus an ghaoth ag síobadh as na ceithre hairde fichead, siúd é ag cóiriú a sheanrothair le gabháil deich míle nó níos mó, suas cnoc agus síos gleann ar na bóithre fliucha fuara.

Ar shiúl leis i mbéal an doininn, a cheann crom aige agus é ag rothaíocht go ládasach. Is minic a fhaigheas an ghaoth a bhuaidh agus caitheann sé siúl, agus ní furast siúl féin, corruair in aimsir sneachta. B'fhéidir go dtabharfadh a rothar suas i lár an iomláin agus go mbeadh sé uair á chóiriú ar thaoibh an bhealaigh mhóir agus gan mórán ama le spáráil aige. Ar aghaidh leis thart le tithe seascaire, doirse foscailte ag cuid acu, solas lách ag soilsiú amach ar an tsráid, ceol agus gáirí agus greann istigh chois tineadh ag lucht airneáil. Ní an madadh tafann, cuireann duine amach a cheann agus maíonn gur creathnach an oíche í ag duine ar bith le a bheith amuigh agus druideann an doras.

An uair a shroiseann sé an scoil sa deireadh, tá sé tuirseach, fuar, fliuch. Tá na solais lasta agus tinidh bhreá thíos fána choinne, agus tá scaifte breá, Gaelach ina suí thart agus leabharthaí nótaí agus pinn luaidhe acu ag fanacht leis. An chuid is óige ag comhrá le chéile i nGaeilig; cuid eile ag foghlaim giota filíochta a bhí le a bheith acu ar a dteangaidh; an chuid is sine ag tabhairt i gceann a chéile na ráití agus na cora cainte a d'fhoghlaim siad an oíche dheireanach.

Stócaigh bhreátha, urrúnta, ionraice ann i ndiaidh a lá a chaitheamh ar na cuibhrinn ag gabháil don bharr, nó ar na buailíocha agus ar na sléibhte i measc an eallaigh agus na gcaorach. Cailíní folláine, feiceálacha ann, iad modhúil, cneasta mar a bhí a máithreachaí rompu. Bróga láidre orthu idir bhuachaillí is chailíní, agus lorg na créafóige ar na bróga céanna. Bíonn siad uilig Gaelach go smior. Murab é go mbíonn, ní thiocfadh siad i ndiaidh a lá cruaidh oibre a dhéanamh isteach go teach scoile chomh múinte, suaimhneach le cupla uair a chur isteach ag coraíocht le briathra agus le díochlaontaí, agus gan iad ag dúil le a dhath saolta a ghnóthú air. Ní bhíonn míníneacht chainte ar bith ag cur as dóibh. Tí siad nach bhfuil ina leithéid sin ach cur i gcéill a foghlaimeadh ón Ghall agus cuireann sé samhnas orthu. Labhrann siad a gcuid Béarla le fuaimeannaí Gaeilge. Aon duine dena ndream a fhéachas le aithris a dhéanamh ar an tSasanach ina chuid cainte, ní bhíonn ann ach amadán, dar leo, nó leathdhuine.

B'fhéidir go sílfeadh duine nach mbeadh eolach orthu go bhfuil cuma gharbh orthu, go bhfuil dóigheannaí garbha leo, go bhfuil greann garbh iontu. Ach tá croí chomh fial, flaithiúil, agus nádúir chomh caoin, cneasta ar chúl an gharbhadais sin agus atá le fáil ar dhroim an domhain.

Bíonn doicheall orthu roimh an strainséir, ar ndóigh, agus bheirtear *inferiority complex* air sin; ach nach beag an t-iontas sin i ndiaidh iad a bheith faoi dhaorsmacht leis na céadtaí bliain.

Má bhíonn fuacht ar an mhúinteoir taistil i ndiaidh a theacht isteach as an doineann, ní bhíonn sé i bhfad ag téamh i measc scaifte mar sin. Is furast Gaeilig a theagasc do rang den tseort óir ní fhaca mé aon duine riamh a raibh fonn air Gaeilig a fhoghlaim nár fhoghlaim í. Téann na cupla uair thart go gasta – róghasta, dar leis an mhúinteoir agus lena chuid scoláirí. Bíonn oiread rudaí le déanamh, tá a fhios agat, le cois na ngnáthcheachtann. Bíonn focla Gaeilge atá fágtha sa Bhéarla sa cheantar le cruinniú, le scríobh síos agus le míniú. Is annamh oíche nach mbíonn dornán de na focla sin leo chuig an mhúinteoir, agus ansin bíonn ainmneacha na mbailte talaimh, na lochann, na n-aibhneacha srl. thart timpeall le míniú. Scéaltaí béaloidis ó na seandaoine le hinse acu.

B'fhéidir go dtiocfadh seanduine isteach i ndiaidh am ranga corroíche go n-inseochadh sé an méid eolais atá aige féin fán tseantsaol sa cheantar agus bród air á fheiceáil á scríobh síos; bród air go bhfuilthear ag cur suime i saol na nGael arís – an t-*inferiority complex* ag imeacht uaidh de réir a chéile agus fíorchroí na nGael á thaispeáint aige!

Éisteann an duine bocht leis an rang ag ceol na seanamhrán i dteangaidh a athara agus tig loinnir ina dhá shúil. Tí sé iad ag déanamh na ndamhsaí Gaelacha, na damhsaí atá ag cur lena nádúir, agus tig bród air, agus toisíonn sé a dh'inse fá bhainiseachaí a chonaic sé amuigh i gcuibhrinn ghlasa fada ó shin, agus daimhseoirí maithe a chonaic sé ag coimhlint le chéile ann.

Tig bean bhreá, lách isteach le braon tae chuig an mhúinteoir, 'braon a bhéarfas chun an bhaile thú,' mar a deir sí féin.

Tá an oíche ag socrú, tá an ghealach ar an aer. Baineann an múinteoir taistil an baile amach ar a sheanrothar. Téann sé thart le tithe a bhfuil an solas as iontu. Tá sé róchleachtaithe leis an oíche le eagla a bheith air roimh thaibhsí. Tá a chóta mór trom, fliuch ach tá a chroí éadrom, agus tá bród air as féin. Títear dó go bhfuil sé ag saothrú a bheatha go cruaidh, ionraice agus go bhfuil a chuid oibre ag tógáil na nGael as an eabar arís. *An tUltach* (Nollaig 2005) 6–7.

70 *An Claidheamh Soluis* (3/11/1906, 9). *First class by LOT An Claidheamh Soluis* (17/11/1906, 9).

71 *Dundalk Democrat* (1/12/1906, 6).

72 *The Anglo-Celt* (17/11/06, 7).

73 *The Anglo-Celt* (24/11/1906, 7).

74 *The Anglo-Celt* (15/12/1906, 7).

75 *The Anglo-Celt* (29/12/1906, 4).

76 *About a hundred students muster on class nights in Cluain Eois, where an tAthair Mac Conmidhe captains the hosts of the Gaels. Lorcán Ó Tuathail, the Múinteoir Taistil, is receiving valuable assistance from Alasdair Mac Néill, N.T. The Craobh has started a dancing class and meditates the formation of a football club. An Claidheamh Soluis* (19/1/1907, 9).

In Muineachán

The report of Labhras Ó Tuathail, Múinteoir taistil, to the recent monthly meeting of the North Muineachán Coiste Ceanntair showed that he had paid thirty-two visits to schools during the month in addition to conducting the Teachers' Classes at the various centres. An Claidheamh Soluis (9/2/1907, 9).

In Oirghialla

The attendance on class-nights is often quite a hundred, an tAthair Séamus and Alastair Mac Néill rendering efficient help to Lorcán Ó Tuathail, the Múinteoir Taistil. An Claidheamh Soluis (16/2/1907, 9).

77 Féach, fosta: sub Oirghialla *An Claidheamh Soluis* (9/3/1907, 9).
sub In Oirghialla – Cluain Eois craobh *An Claidheamh Soluis* (27/4/1907, 9).

Aghabog – Classes were held at the hall of the Craobh in Leacht na mBard, as usual, last week. On Wednesday the attendance was very good, there being 30 cailíní and 40 buachaillí present. The Múinteoir Taistil, Lorcán Ua Tuathail, was unable to attend on Wednesday as he is suffering from a severe cold. Anglo-Celt (29/12/1906, 4).

78 Thug sé cuairt amháin ar Mhuineachán i ndiaidh dó imeacht go Baile Átha Cliath. *Mr. Lorcán Ua Tuathail, late múinteoir taistil, paid a flying visit to the district (i.e. North Monaghan). Dundalk Democrat* (21/9/1907, 16).

79 *Freeman's Journal* (25/7/1907, 10).

80 *Freeman's Journal* (7/9/1907, 17).

81 *An Claidheamh Soluis* (14/9/1907, 9).

82 *Freeman's Journal* (4/10/1907, 5). Píosa ina dhiaidh sin faoi chúrsaí Gaeilge san áit. Tá mé buíoch de Dhara Folan as an tagairt seo a chur ar mo shúile.

Foilsíodh nótaí eile faoina chuid oibre ina dhiaidh sin.

In Cuala

*At a meeting of Coiste Chomhairle Uí Chualainn held in Shankill on Sunday 29*th *inst., Seaghan Ua Reagain, Uachdaran, in the chair, a report was handed in by Lorcán Ua Tuathail, the Múinteoir Taistil for the district, showing that Irish is now taught by him in every one of the schools in Canon O'Hea's parish for two hours weekly. The teacher at Cornelscourt teaches Irish himself. The Múinteoir Taistil is also* *teaching in the Booterstown Girls' Schools (Sisters of Mercy). An Claidheamh Soluis* (12/10/1907, 8).

In Cuala

At its recent meeting the Coiste Comhairle here welcomed the announcement that Canon Murray, P.P., would co-operate in the introduction of Irish in the Dalkey schools. The Múinteoir Taistil, Lorcán Ó Tuathail, reported that his time was now fully occupied by class work in school and branch. Especially encouraging was the progress in Dun Laoghaire and Deilginis. An Claidheamh Soluis (16/11/1907, 8).

83 *An Claidheamh Soluis* (12/10/ 1907).

84 *An Claidheamh Soluis* (18/1/ 1908).

85 *An Claidheamh Soluis* (18/1/1908, 11).

86 *Freeman's Journal* (10/1/1908, 6).

87 Luaite in ainm.ie.

88 *Freeman's Journal* (15/9/1908, 3).

89 *An Claidheamh Soluis* (6/2/1909, 4)

90 *An Claidheamh Soluis* (6/2/1909, 6)

91 *Irish Independent* (2/2/1909, 4).

LÁ AN CHÍOSA

Dráma a chum

Labhrás Ó Tuathail

An Fhoireann:

Manders (Tiarna Talún)

Siobhán (Bean Manders)

Tomás Cleiteach (Cléireach Manders)

Conchúr (An Báille)

Máire

Micheál Réidh

Páidín Gabha

Maighréad Ní Chrónáin

Seán Dubh

Micheál Réamach

Diarmaid Ó Máille

Seán Ó Murchú (Cleasaí an Pharóiste)

Seán Pháidín Gabha

Bríd Réidh (Deirfiúr Mhichíl)

Agus daoine eile.

Áit: Oifig an Chíosa

Manders agus Tomás Cleiteach ar láthair.

MANDERS: Nach caillte an scéal é mise a bheith ag fuireach leis na tionóntaí mallaithe seo! An gceapann siad nach bhfuil aon bhlas eile le déanamh agam? Tá mé ag fanacht anois ar feadh uair an chloig agus níor tháinig fós ach beirt nó triúr; ach bhéarfad deich nóiméad eile dóibh agus mura mbeidh siad anseo an uair sin socróidh mise iad. *(Leis an gcléireach).* Bí ag fáil réidh na bpáipéar sin. Dar fia, beidh athrú scéil ag na rógairí úd ar ball. *(Ag glaoch ar Chonchúr an báille).* Ar fhógair tú an cíos ar na tionóntaí?

CONCHÚR: D'fhógras, a mháistir. *(Ag umhlú don mháistir).*

MANDERS: Gabh amach anois is féach an bhfuil aon chosúlacht teachta orthu.

Téann Conchúr amach.

MANDERS *(Leis féin):* Cén dochar, ach beidh siad ag iarraidh lascaine ar ball chomh teann is dá mbeidís anseo in am; ach gheobhaidh siad laghdú nó lascaine i gcaoi éigin eile go luath.

Tig Conchúr isteach.

CONCHÚR: Tá siad ag teacht, a mháistir.

MANDERS: Ba é sin a leas; ní raibh acu ach cúpla nóiméad eile.

Tá na tionóntaí cruinnithe taobh amuigh den doras, iad uile ach Micheál Réidh.

MANDERS *(Leis an gcéad fhear):* Cén t-ainm atá ortsa?

AN CHÉAD FHEAR: Páidín Gabha an t-ainm agus an sloinne atá ormsa.

MANDERS *(Leis an gcléireach):* Cén cíos atá ar Pháidín Gabha, a Thomáis?

TOMÁS: Tá, cíos bliana. Sin £8 atá le n-íoc aige.

MANDERS *(Le Páidín):* Leag £8 anseo ar an mbord agam, go beo tapaidh.

PÁIDÍN: Seo dhuit, an méid airgid atá agam. *(Ag fágáil an airgid ar an mbord).*

MANDERS *(Tar éis é a chomhaireamh):* Ní dhéanfaidh sé seo, a Pháidín, tá tú punt gearr.

PÁIDÍN: Níl neart agam air. B'fhéidir go ndeachaigh sé go han-chrua orm an méid sin féin a bhailiú duit. Bhí mé ar mo lándícheall d'oíche agus de ló, moch agus déanach, ag iarraidh airgead a dhéanamh amach as talamh shuaite, shuarach, a bheadh daor go leor orm dá bhfaighinn in aisce é.

MANDERS: Éist do bhéal! Tá faitíos orm go mbeidh tú suite sa bpríosún fós, mura bhfuil ag Dia. Cén uair a bheas an punt sin agat dom?

PÁIDÍN: Ráithe ón lá inniu, má bhím beo, le cúnamh Dé.

CONCHÚR *(Ar leataobh le Manders):* Ná creid focal ón bhfalsóir bradach sin. Tá sé thíos ina phóca ag an rógaire. Mise mo bhannaí go mbeidh luach an óil ar ball aige. Creid mé, má ghéilleann tú dó, go mbeidh chuile dhiabhal eile gearr mar an gcéanna.

MANDERS: Dar fia, a Chonchúir, is maith a rinne tú é sin a chur in iúl dom. *(Le Páidín).* Seo, cuir an méid seo san áit ar chuir tú an punt agus cloisfidh tú uaimse i gceann seachtaine, a bhuachaill!

PÁIDÍN: B'fhéidir gur fearr duit é a ghlacadh. An gcuala tú riamh é 'is fearr éan ar do bhois ná cor ar chairde?'

MANDERS: Bí ag imeacht, a bhithiúnaigh! *(Go feargach).* A Chonchúir, tiomáin isteach tionónta eile chugam go deifreach.

Tig tionónta mná isteach.

MANDERS: Cén t-ainm atá ortsa, le do thoil, a bhean chóir?

AN BHEAN: Tá, Maighréad Ní Chrónáin.

MANDERS *(Le Tomás):* Cé mhéad cíosa atá ar Mhaighréad Ní Chrónáin?

AN CLÉIREACH: Tá, cíos bliana agus leathbhliain ráta (ráthach sa LS.) – sin £9 ar fad.

MAIGHRÉAD: Tá sin orm gan amhras, ach faraor géar, níl sé agam. Baintreach bhocht mise. Ó íocadh an cíos cheana leat cailleadh mo Liam bocht, an fear ab fhearr agus ba chneasta sa bparóiste, go ndéana Dia trócaire ar a anam. Buaileadh leis an eitinn amplach é tá leathbhliain ó shin agus níor fhág sé an teach gur fhág sé ins an gclár é. Mharaigh sé é féin ag iarraidh an cíos a dhéanamh amach duitse.

MANDERS: Nach bhfuil sé imithe anois agus cén mhaith a bheith ag caint air? Amach leis an gcíos, má tá sé agat.

MAIGHRÉAD: Níl sé agam nó go ndíolfad cúpla uan atá agam i gceann míosa nó mar sin.

Téann Conchúr anonn go dtí an áit a bhfuil Manders, ag cogarnach ina chluais.

MANDERS: Go raibh maith agat. Tá loilíoch mhaith in do sheilbh faoi láthair. Tabhair leat chuig aonach an Spidéil í arú amárach agus beidh an cíos agat ansin.

MAIGHRÉAD: Cad a dhéanfadh na páistí bochta ansin? Ní bheadh bolgam bainne acu le cur ina mbéal.

MANDERS: Is cuma liom.

MAIGHRÉAD *(Ag imeacht go brónach amach):* Nár ba chuma le Dia sin!

Tig fear eile isteach.

AN FEAR: Is mise Diarmaid Ó Máille as Baile na gCearc.

MANDERS (*Le Tomás*): Cé mhéad cíosa atá ar Dhiarmaid Ó Máille?

TOMÁS: Tá, cíos bliana, a mháistir. Sin sé phunt coróin.

Íocann Diarmaid £6 5s.

DIARMAID: Tabhair dom lascaine anois, a mháistir! Tá muirín mhór orm.

MANDERS: Muirín! Tá muirín mhór orm féin. An measann tú an anuas as an spéir a thagann bia nó deoch chugam ach an oiread leatsa? Fág sin uaim – tá deifir orm!

DIARMAID (*Ag imeacht amach*): Dona go leor!

Tig tionónta eile isteach.

MANDERS: Cén t-ainm atá ortsa, a dhuine chóir?

AN TIONÓNTA: De Mhuintir Réamach mise, a mháistir.

MANDERS: Cén t-ainm baiste a thug siad ort? Nó ar baistíodh thú ar chor ar bith?

MICHEÁL RÉAMACH: Baistíodh gan amhras. Micheál a ghlaoitear orm.

TOMÁS: Tá deich bpunt le n-íoc agat, a Mhichíl.

Íocann Micheál amach deich bpunt.

MANDERS: B'fhéidir go bhfuil muirín eile ortsa, a Mhichíl, agus go dteastódh lascaine uait?

MICHEÁL: Dar fia! De réir cosúlachta is beag an mhaith rud ar bith a iarraidh ortsa.

Déanann Manders gáire.

MANDERS (*Le tionónta eile*): Cén t-ainm atá ortsa?

AN TIONÓNTA: Seán Dubh.

MANDERS: Sin leasainm, tá mé ag ceapadh.

SEÁN DUBH: Ó, gabhaim pardún agat, a mháistir. Sin leasainm atá ag na comharsana orm ó d'fhás an fhéasóg mhór, dhubh seo ar m'éadan. Is é Seán Ó Conghaile m'ainm ceart.

MANDERS: Cé mhéad atá ag Seán Ó Conghaile le n-íoc, a Thomáis?

AN CLÉIREACH: Tá dhá phunt déag aige le n-íoc, a mháistir.

SEÁN DUBH *(Tar éis an cíos a íoc):* Tabhair dom lascaine anois, a mháistir. Tá a fhios agat go maith go bhfuil an saol go han-dona fá láthair; nach fiú trácht ar a bhfuil le fáil ar stoic agus, maidir leis na fataí, ní fiú iad a bhaint.

MANDERS *(Go feargach):* Bí ag imeacht as m'amharc, is bí buíoch nach é an cíos a d'ardaigh mé ort i leaba lascaine nó laghdú a thabhairt duit!

SEÁN DUBH: Dá n-ardófá féin, ní hé do chéad uair sin a dhéanamh. D'ardaigh tú orm é nuair a réidh mé Gort na nDriseog ó bhun go barr. Ar m'fhocal, is cráite an scéal é! Ba cheart dúinn a bheith go han-bhuíoch díot gur fhág tú sinn beo ar chor ar bith. Ach más olc an maol, is seacht measa an mullach. Seo é an bithiúnach *(ag bagairt ar Chonchúr)* is ciontach leis an méid léin agus scrios a d'éirigh do na tionóntaí ar do dhúthaigh – a d'fhág na copóga sráide ag fás ar lorg na dtithe a bhí te, téagarach agus a d'fhág an bhaintreach agus an dílleachta ar leataobh an bhóthair. Ach buíochas le Dia go bhfuil an lá ag breacadh agus na néalta ag glanadh – an lá a mbeidh talamh na tíre ag muintir na tíre arís agus nach mbeidh aon chall acu a dhul chugatsa ná chuig do leithéide ag iarraidh lascaine nó laghdú ina gcuid cíosa.

Imíonn sé go dtí an doras agus fanann sé ag féachaint ar Manders.

MANDERS *(go hard):* Tá tú tráthúil go leor, a mhic ó, go bhfuil admháil do chíosa in do phóca agat, nó bheadh athrú scéil agat amárach. *(Ag smaoineamh).* Ach ina dhiaidh sin, ní tú is ciontach ach na bithiúnaigh bhradacha seo atá ag dul thart ar fud na tíre ag cur mearbhaill ortsa is do leithéid lena gcuid cainte. *(Ag suí síos).* Ins an bpríosún ba cheart dóibh a bheith.

Nuair atá an cíos íoctha acu go léir, fiafraíonn Manders an bhfaca ceachtar acu Micheál Réidh.

DIARMAID Ó MÁILLE: Chonaic mise inné é, a mháistir, agus sílim nach raibh sé go rómhaith le slaghdán.

MANDERS: Ar labhair sé faoi chíos nó rud ar bith mar sin?

DIARMAID: Níor labhair; ach, murar labhair féin, sílim nach raibh cíos ag an duine bocht.

MANDERS: Mura bhfuil sé anois aige, ná raibh sé go brách aige.

Imíonn na tionóntaí amach.

MANDERS *(Ag glaoch ar an mbáille):* A Chonchúir, ar fhógair tú an cíos ar Mhicheál Réidh?

CONCHÚR: D'fhógras, a mháistir, ach is é a dúirt sé liom gur ag cur aistir orm féin a bhí mé gan dada dá bharr agam – nach é an cíos a bhí ag cur imní air.

MANDERS: Cén leithscéal a thug sé uaidh?

CONCHÚR: Níor fhéadas aon cheart a bhaint de, a mháistir. Bhí sé chomh drochmhúinte le seanmhúille. Nuair a d'fhiafraíos an raibh an cíos bailithe aige is é a dúirt sé liom go feargach: "Ná bí do mo bhodhrú; cá bhfaighinnse airgead le haghaidh cíos? An measann tú," ar seisean, "an as na clocha a gheobhainn é?" Ach ní raibh brí ar bith ins an méid sin. Dúirt sé go raibh mé ag cur tinneas cinn air agus leis sin chuaigh sé anonn go dtí an tinteán agus tharraing sé amach an tlú. "Anois", a deir sé, "mura dté tú amach go tapaidh gheobhaidh tú leadóg den tlú seo anuas ar mhullach do chinn agus b'fhéidir nach mbeadh an oiread sin deifir ort ag teacht anseo arís". Ar chaoi ar bith mura mbeadh chomh tapaidh is a chuaigh mé amach ní anseo a bheinn inniu.

MANDERS: An mbíonn sé ag ól anois?

CONCHÚR: Ól, an ea? D'ólfadh sé an chloch íochtair! Maidir le ól, tá faitíos orm nach stadfaidh sé go brách de.

Imíonn Conchúr amach.

MANDERS *(Go feargach leis féin):* Níl rógaire beirthe inniu chomh mór le Micheál Réidh; ach is gearr a bheas sé ag déanamh beartaíocht ormsa. *(Leis an gCléireach).* An bhfuil an páipéar sin líonta agat?

TOMÁS: Tá, a mháistir, ach a ainm a chur air.

MANDERS: Déan deifir! Cuirfidh mise teachtaire chuige anois, nach gcuirfidh sé amach le tlú!

Tig Micheál isteach, a hata ina láimh aige agus é ag féachaint go han-bhrónach.

MICHEÁL: Go mbeannaí Dia anseo.

MANDERS: Hó, hó, tháinig tú faoi dheireadh. An bhfuil an cíos agat anois féin?

MICHEÁL: Níl.

MANDERS (*Go hard*): Tuige?

MICHEÁL: Bhí mo bhean bhocht tinn ó shin agus cuid de mo chuid páistí. Bhí trí nó ceathair de mhuca beaga agam agus b'éigean dom iad a dhíol le haghaidh purgóid agus dochtúir a thabhairt dóibh, agus leis an scéal a dhéanamh níos measa, chaith mé féin sé seachtainí in mo luí ar chúl mo dhroma gan blas a ithe agus d'ólfainn an donas!

MANDERS: Creidim thú ansin ar chuma ar bith.

MICHEÁL: Má ligfidh tú an bhliain seo liom, a mháistir, is mé an chéad fhear a íocfas thú an bhliain seo chugainn, má bhím beo in mo shláinte, le cúnamh Dé.

MANDERS: Ná síl gur amadán atá ionamsa ar chor ar bith. Nuair a théim isteach don bhaile mór lá aonaigh nó margaidh feicim thú ar meisce.

MICHEÁL: An mise, a mháistir? Sílim go bhfuil tú ag dul amú. Duine éigin eile a chonaic tú mar nár ól mise deoir le ráithe, mar gheall ar mo bhean agus mo chuid páistí.

MANDERS: Anois, a Mhichíl righin, réidh, lig [le] do chuid steallabhréag domsa mar nach dtógfaidh mise uait iad. Tá cáil ort ar fud na tíre nach bhfuil tú ag déanamh blas ach poitín, is á ól, agus mise gan mo chuid cíosa. Ach ní sháróidh do chuid bladaireachta mise. *(Go feargach).* Mura mbeidh an cíos agat domsa tráthnóna an lae amárach beidh tú amuigh ar an mbóthar faoi cheann coicíse, chomh cinnte is atá ainm Micheál Réidh mar ainm ort.

MICHEÁL: Geallaim duit anois go fírinneach nach n-ólfaidh mé deoir arís go brách agus go gcuirfidh mé suas chuile phingin de mo shaothrú chun an cíos a thabhairt duitse, má bheidh an oiread sin foighde agat.

MANDERS: Éist, a phótaire shuaraigh! Is iomaí geall a thug tú uait i rith do shaoil, agus níor choinnigh tú iad. Ar an ábhar sin níl súil agam go gcoinneofá do gheall liomsa.

MICHEÁL: Cé a d'inis duit é sin, an bhfuil dochar é a fhiafraí?

MANDERS: Nach cuma duit?

MICHEÁL *(Ag bualadh a dhoirn ar an mbord):* Níor thug mise aon gheall riamh nár choinnigh mé.

MANDERS: A Mhichíl shúgaigh, tá mé ag éisteacht leat anois le fada agus ag dul i ndonacht atáir; ach mar a deir an seanrá: "Chomh fada is a ritheas an sionnach béarfar air faoi dheireadh".

Tig Siobhán aniar as an seomra tar éis an torann ar an mbord a chloisint. Iarrann Micheál pardún mar a leanas:

MICHEÁL: A bhean uasal, ó tharla gur máthair chlainne thú féin, agus go bhfuil a fhios agat chomh deacair is atá sé iad a bheathú, iarraim mar impí agus mar achainí ort mo phardún a fháil ó d'fhear uasal, onórach, agus gan mé féin agus mo mhuirín bhocht, lag a chur amach ar an mbóthar.

SIOBHÁN: Lig leis an bhliain seo agus íocfaidh sé thú an chéad bhliain eile. Nach n-íocfaidh, a Mhichíl?

MICHEÁL: M'anam go n-íocfad, le cúnamh Dé. Go bhfága Dia i bhfad os cionn do mhuirín thú, a bhean uasal, charthanach, ghrásúil, agus go mba seacht míle fearr a bheas tú bliain ó inniu.

Téann Micheál amach agus glaonn Manders air.

MANDERS: Ná himigh chomh tapaidh sin, a Mhichíl Réidh. Níl mise réidh leat fós; ná síl é. *(Déanann sé smaoineamh ar feadh tamaill bhig leis féin).* Drochrath air! Ní maith liom mo bhean a eiteach. Ach m'anam nach mbeidh mé gan mo chíos, má fhéadaim.

MICHEÁL: Cad eile, a mháistir?

MANDERS: Tá trí cheist agam le cur chugat agus má fhreagróidh tú iad, ní amháin go maithfidh mé an bhliain seo thú, ach beidh do thalamh saor ó chíos arís go brách agat.

MICHEÁL: Agus cad iad na trí cheist, a mháistir?

MANDERS: Seo iad na trí cheist – cén meáchan atá ins an ngealaigh? Cé mhéad réalt sa spéir? Agus cad tá mé ag ceapadh nó ag cuimhneamh air in m'intinn?

MICHEÁL: Muise, ob, ob, ú! Nach bhfuil ceisteanna níos réidhe ná iad sin le tabhairt dom? *(Leis féin).* Aililiú! Meáchan na gealaí, an méid réalt sa spéir agus cad tá sé ag cuimhneamh air!

MANDERS: Imigh leat anois, agus bíodh freagraí na gceist sin ar bharr do theangan ag a cúig a chlog tráthnóna an lae inniu.

MICHEÁL *(Ag dul amach):* Ní fhéadfadh an scéal a bheith níos measa.

Téann Siobhán siar sa seomra. Cuireann fear óg a chloigeann isteach an doras.

MANDERS *(leis an gCléireach):* Cé hé sin ag an doras? Ar ndóigh, ní tionónta é?

AN FEAR: Murab ea, is mac tionónta mé. Is mise Seán Gabha, mac Pháidín Gabha, as Troscadh na gCapall. An bhfuil aithne agat air?

MANDERS: Tá, faraor! Agus cad a thug thusa anseo?

SEÁN: Ag ceapadh go dtógfá an cíos a d'eitigh tú m'athair faoi tamall ó shin.

MANDERS: Níor thóg mé ó d'athair é agus tógfaidh mé uaitse é! Bí ag imeacht, a charracháin!

SEÁN: Ní thógfaidh tú uaimse é; diabhal mise mura dtógfaidh tú ar an mball *(Ag bagairt a chinn).*

Imíonn Seán amach tar éis féachaint go géar ar Manders agus ar an mBáille.

MANDERS *(Le Tomás):* Cad é sin a dúirt sé ag dul amach dó?

TOMÁS: Ní hé a bheannacht a thug sé duit ar chuma ar bith.

MANDERS: B'fhearr liomsa a mhallacht ná a bheannacht. Ach bhí míniú níos measa ná sin ina chuid goithí. *(Tar éis smaoineamh ar feadh tamaill).* Dar fia, is cosúil go gcaithfidh mé aire mhaith a thabhairt dom féin feasta.

Tig Siobhán aniar as an seomra.

SIOBHÁN: Seo, a Thomáis, tabhair an leabhar seo go teach an tsagairt. Fuair mé ar iasacht coicís nó trí seachtainí ó shin uaidh é. Abair leis go bhfuil mé go han-bhuíoch de ar a shon ach ná lig ort féin go bhfuil mise ins an mbaile mór inniu. *(Lena fear).* Tá cáil ar an gcléireach go bhfuil sé rud beag cabach agus sin leithscéal a bhí agam é a chur amú. Inis dom anois ar chreid tusa an méid a dúirt Conchúr leat i dtaobh Mhichíl Réidh? Chuala mise chuile fhocal a tháinig amach as a bhéal.

MANDERS: Chreid, gan amhras.

SIOBHÁN: Ní raibh an cneamhaire sin ach ag stealladh bréag leat. Sílimse go bhfuil Conchúr ag oibriú leis an iomarca dúthrachta ag iarraidh ort Micheál Réidh agus a mhuirín bhocht a chur amach ar an mbóthar mar chuir sé in iúl duit cheana go minic daoine bochta a chur amach nuair a bheadh a gcuid talún ag teastáil uaidh féin nó ó chuid dá dhaoine muinteartha. Nach bhfuil feilm Mharcais Seoighe - an fheilm is mó, agus an talamh is saibhre in do dhúthaigh aige féin; agus nach bhfuil feilm an Bhúrcaigh ag a dheartháir – an fheilm is gaire dó i méid agus i saibhreas?

MANDERS: Bhí an oiread sin Búrcach ar mo dhúthaigh fadó, nach gcuimhním cé air a bhfuil tú ag trácht.

SIOBHÁN: Is ar Mháirtín Rua de Búrca a bhí i nGoirtín na Gréine fadó. Nach gcuimhníonn tú air?

MANDERS *(Ag cuimilt a chinn):* Ní chuimhním.

SIOBHÁN: Nach gcuimhníonn tú ar an bhfear a bhfuair a bhean bás cois claí an lá a chuir tú amach iad gan cleith os a gcionn ach an spéir ghorm?

MANDERS: Ó, cuimhním, cuimhním, agus tá aiféala orm anois, nuair atá sé déanach. Agus cuimhním, freisin, gurbh é an Conchúr céanna, lena chuid beartaíochta agus bréag, ba chiontach leis.

SIOBHÁN: Tá a fhios agam go maith nach féidir leat an méid éagóra a rinne tú a thabhairt ar ais, ach tá a fhios agam go bhfuil sé in do chumas cúiteamh, nó leorghníomh a dhéanamh. Ná dún do shúil ar na tionóntaí bochta a chuir tú amach, atá ina gcónaí i mbotháin bheaga, shuaracha timpeall na háite seo ag faire go grámhar ar na seanbhallaí agus ar lorg na dtithe inar rugadh iad, ag súil go bhfosclódh Dia bearna dóibh fós agus go gcuirfeadh Dia in do chroíse an talamh a thabhairt ar ais dóibh as ar dhíbir tú iad!

Glac mo chomhairle. Díol amach do chuid talún agus socraigh leis na daoine bochta seo.

MANDERS: A Shiobhán, níl ach iomlán na fírinne in do chuid cainte. Nach orm a bhí mí-ádh an domhain go léir a bheith ag caint ar mo dhonas agus ar mo dhrochghníomha mar gheall ar an rógaire bradach sin! Glacfaidh mé do chomhairle; díolfaidh mé amach mo chuid talún leis na tionóntaí agus socród ar ais ar a gcuid talún féin an méid a bhfuil beo de na daoine bochta seo a chuir mé amach ar dhroch-chomhairle Chonchúir. Anois, beidh Micheál Réidh anseo ag a cúig a chlog le freagra na dtrí cheist a chuir mé air. Ach, go deimhin, mura mbeidh siad aige féin, ní bheidh mé ródhian ar an gcréatúr. Cuirfidh mé scéal ina dhiaidh sin chuig na tionóntaí a bheith anseo ins an am chéanna mar tá cúpla focal agam le rá leo.

MANDERS (*Le Máire, an cailín aimsire, a bhí ag séideadh na tine, ag glanadh an tinteáin srl. an fhaid a bhí an comhrá ar siúl):* A Mháire, má thagann aon duine anseo ag tóraíocht scéalta nó ag piocadh asatsa, ná tabhair aon aird orthu; seachain ar chraiceann do chluaise an inseofá ní ar bith faoi na trí cheist, nó faoin ngnó beag sin a bhí idir mé féin agus Micheál Réidh.

MÁIRE: Ára, tuige a n-inseoinn rud ar bith mar sin? Nach bog mé! Níl baint ná páirt ag Máire le gnó duine ar bith ach lena gnó féin. Ní bhfuair fear ná bean ná páiste lorg mo theangansa riamh.

MANDERS: Is maith an cailín. Anois, rachaidh mé féin agus Siobhán amach ag spaisteoireacht agus má thagann Micheál Réidh anseo romhainn, abair leis fanacht – nach mbeidh mé i bhfad amuigh. *(Leis féin).* Ní dhéanfaidh an méid sin comhairle dochar ar bith, mar tá an tubaiste go deo ar theanga mná.

Imíonn sé amach. Téann Máire anonn go dtí an doras. Féachann sí amach.

MÁIRE *(Léi féin):* Dar fia! Is dona atá an saol má chaithfidh mé mo theanga a choinneáil in mo phluic gan fhios tuige; gan cead agam labhairt le éinne is mian liom. M'anamsa gur dona! Ní an oiread sin de shaibhreas atá dá bharr agam, go mbeinn chomh cúramach faoi. Má tá sé ina dhuine uasal chomh mór sin nach breá nach é a lámh a chuirfeadh sé ina phóca is a rá go breá, fiúntach: "Seo, a Mháire, rud éigin ar fónamh duit", tar éis lán mála d'airgead a fháil.

Tig Seán Ó Murchú, Bríd Réidh agus comharsana eile isteach.

SEÁN Ó MURCHÚ: Go mbeannaí Dia anseo!

MÁIRE: Go mbeannaí Dia agus Máire duit! Cén scéal é, a Sheáin?

SEÁN: Dheamhan barr nuachta! Féachaint an raibh Manders istigh a bhí mé, mar bhí gnóthaí beaga agam de.

MÁIRE: Tá sé tar éis imeacht amach; ba cheart go gcasfadh sé duit ar an mbóthar.

SEÁN: Is é a chonaic mé ag dul síos an bóthar, mar sin.

MÁIRE: Má chonaic tú duine ar bith, is é.

SEÁN: An raibh Micheál Réidh anseo ó shin?

MÁIRE: Dar m'fhocal, bhí. Chaith sé féin agus an Máistir tamall maith ag caint agus an Máistir ag cur go leor ceisteanna crua air, dar liomsa. Níl a fhios agam cad a bhí siad a rá, ach chualas cúpla focal a dúirt Micheál bocht ag dul amach dó, is é sin 'nach bhféadfadh an chúis a bheith níos measa'.

SEÁN BÁN (*Comharsa*): Tá trioblóid éigin ar an duine bocht mar sin.

BRÍD RÉIDH: Tá faitíos orm go bhfuil mar nár stad mé ar feadh na hoíche aréir ach ag brionglóid air.

SEÁN Ó MURCHÚ: Ná cuir suim ar bith i mbrionglóid. Bhí mise uair ag brionglóid go raibh mé ag déanamh créafóige ins an talamh agus seachtain ón lá sin bhí mé féin agus Peigse Ní Eidhin pósta le chéile!

BRÍD: Is é an faitíos is mó a bheadh ormsa, nuair a bheadh gloine ólta aige go mbeadh sé drochmhúinte leis an Máistir agus b'fhéidir gurb é a bhualadh a dhéanfadh sé.

SEÁN Ó MURCHÚ *(ag gáirí):* Muise, go dtuga Dia ciall duit, a Bhríd. Tá baol mór air é sin a dhéanamh. Ní bheadh aingeal as an bhflaitheas ag féachaint chomh naofa ná chomh simplí le Micheál Réidh nuair a bheadh sé ag caint le Manders nó lena mhnaoi.

BRÍD: B'fhéidir sin; ach nach cuimhneach leat an oíche úd tar éis Micheál a theacht abhaile ó Aonach Chnoc an Daláin, tharla go dtáinig cúpla focal idir é féin agus Paits Shéamais. D'éirigh Micheál de léim agus é ar buile agus mura mbeadh go ndeachaigh Seán Dubh anseo eatarthu, ní bheadh deireadh leis an oíche úd go brách.

SEÁN Ó MURCHÚ: Muise, go dtuga Dia ciall duit, a Bhríd. An bhfuil tusa ag cur Paits Shéamais i gcomórtas le Manders? Níl Micheál Réidh ina amadán chomh mór sin is go gcaillfeadh sé a chloigeann nuair a bheadh sé ag caint le tiarna na talún.

MÁIRE: Más ag ceapadh go n-éireoidh clampar ar bith den tsórt sin do Mhicheál atá sibh, tá sibh ag dul amú go mór, mar nach raibh deoir ina bholg, dar liomsa, ach an oiread le ceachtar agaibhse.

BRÍD: Go mba slán an scéalaí!

Tá torann ag an doras. Tig Micheál isteach.

Ó! Míle buíochas le Dia go dtáinig tú slán ar chaoi ar bith.

SEÁN Ó MURCHÚ: Céad míle fáilte romhat, a Mhichíl. Anois ar an bpointe a bhí muid ag caint ort. *(Leis féin, tar éis féachaint ar Mhicheál)*. M'anam go sílim gur éirigh rud éigin do Mhicheál inniu, mar tá sé ag féachaint go han-bhrónach. *(Le Micheál).* Cén chaoi a d'éirigh an lá leat le Manders?

MICHEÁL *(Go feargach):* Drochrath ar Manders! Tá mo cheann iompaithe aige.

SEÁN Ó MURCHÚ: Tuige, a Mhichíl? Dar fia tá cloigeann maith ort fós *(Ag bualadh a bhoise ar chloigeann Mhichíl agus ag gáirí).*

MICHEÁL: A Sheáin Uí Mhurchú, má tá an t-ádh ort, ná bí ag magadh fúmsa in mo thrioblóid.

BRÍD: Go dtuga Dia ábhar gáirí dúinn!

SEÁN Ó MURCHÚ: Áiméan! Ní le bheith ag magadh fútsa a tháinig mise anseo, ach ó tharla gurb é 'Lá an Chíosa' a bhí ann, tháinig mé ag tóraíocht scéalta.

MICHEÁL: Má fhanann tú le scéalta uaimse, beidh tú gan scéal.

SEÁN Ó MURCHÚ: Cén fáth tú a bheith chomh feargach sin?

MICHEÁL *(Go hard):* Tabhair rud beag suaimhnis dom anois go bhfeice mé cad a dhéanfaidh mé ag an cúig a chlog.

SEÁN Ó MURCHÚ: Níl cruinnithe anseo anocht ach sinn féin, agus inis dúinn cad a dúirt an Máistir leat, más é do thoil é.

MICHEÁL: Tá sé chomh maith agaibh an teach a fhágáil más libh a bheith ag piocadh asamsa mar sin. *(Ag béicíl).* Má iarrfar ceist níos mó orm, bainfidh mé díom mo chóta.

BRÍD: Lig dó, a Sheáin, agus b'fhéidir go n-inseodh sé dá thoil féin ar ball é.

Téann Seán Ó Murchú anonn go dtí an áit a bhfuil Micheál, agus leagann sé lámh ar a ghualainn, agus é ag gáirí.

MICHEÁL *(Ag baint de a chóta):* Mura bhfágfaidh sibh an teach go beo, beidh cuimhne ar an oíche anocht!

Ritheann cuid acu amach le teann faitís.

BRÍD: Ó tharla go bhfuil siad imithe anois ach beirt nó triúr, cén dochar a dhéanfaidh sé duit é a insint?

MICHEÁL: Ní dhéanfaidh ná maith ach an oiread.

BRÍD: Agus más maith nó olc é, nach gcloisfimid faoi dheireadh é?

MICHEÁL *(Go ciúin):* Ó tharla go ndeachaigh sibh orm chomh crua sin, inseoidh mé daoibh cad a dúirt Manders liom ar chuma ar bith. Dúirt sé nach mbeadh teach os mo chionn mura mbeinn in ann trí cheist a chuir sé orm a fhreagairt dó. Seo iad na trí cheist – an chéad cheist, cén meáchan atá ar an ngealaigh; an dara ceist, cé mhéad réalt sa spéir; an tríú ceist, cad tá sé ag cuimhneamh air ina intinn?

SEÁN *(Tar éis smaoineamh):* Agus is iad seo a chuir an oiread sin feirge ort! Ná bíodh imní ar bith ort. Deirtear nach bhfuil cleasaí eile ins an bparóiste mar mé féin, agus nach bhfuil diabhalacht ar bith ag dul uaim, agus bain an chloigeann díom mura n-imreoidh mé beart ar Manders, pé in Éirinn é. Chun tosnú ar an gcéad cheist, chualas riamh go raibh ceithre ceathrúna ins an ngealaigh; faoin dara ceist, chualas Máirtín Eilís ag rá lá go ndúirt an máistir scoile leis – agus ná iarr ina dhiaidh sin é – go raibh ocht milliún ceithre mhíle dhéag go leith réalt sa spéir; agus i dtaobh na tríú ceiste, is furasta a insint do Mhanders cad tá sé ag cuimhneamh air ina intinn.

MICHEÁL: Cén chaoi?

SEÁN: An chaoi seo. Níl ortsa ach do chóta agus do hata a thabhairt domsa. Is é an sórt bríste céanna atá orainn. Ansin cad tá agamsa le déanamh ach féasóg eile a chur ar m'éadan, mar an ceann atá ortsa. Beimid ansin mar dhá phréachán, ní bheidh aithne ag duine ar bith beo ar Sheán Ó Murchú thar Mhicheál Réidh, nó ar Mhicheál Réidh thar Sheán Ó Murchú. Freagród an chéad cheist agus an dara ceist, mar a dúras leat, agus nuair a fhiafraíonn sé díom cad tá mé ag ceapadh in m'intinn, beidh mé in ann é a fhreagairt mar an gcéanna.

MICHEÁL: Ára, cén sórt freagra a thabharfas tú dó?

SEÁN: Anois, ná labhair focal níos mó ina thimpeall, ach tabhair dom do chóta agus do hata.

Tabharann Micheál a chóta agus a hata do Sheán agus téann Micheál ag tóraíocht féasóige ar fud an bhaile. Imíonn an chuid eile de na comharsana amach. Tig bacach isteach.

AN BACACH: Bail ó Dhia agus ó Mhuire oraibh!

MÁIRE *(Ag féachaint go géar air):* M'anam go sílim go bhfaca mé thusa cheana, a bhuachaill, nó tá mé ag dul amú go mór.

AN BACACH: Má chonaic, ní ins an teach seo é. Ní raibh mé riamh anseo le do linnse.

MÁIRE: Cén t-ainm atá ort? An bhfuil aon dochar é a fhiafraí?

AN BACACH: Níl aon dochar. Séamas Paorach an t-ainm atá ormsa.

MÁIRE: Cá mbíonn tú 'do chónaí?

AN BACACH: Cá mbím 'mo chónaí? Níl áit chónaithe ar bith agamsa, faraor, ach mé ag imeacht 'mo chréatúr bhocht ar fud na tíre ag tóraíocht leapa agus ruainne le n-ithe. Más mian leat fios a bheith agat air, rugadh agus tógadh go gnaíúil mé i mBóithrín na Sliogán. An bhfuil an duine uasal seo istigh?

MÁIRE: Níl, agus sílim gur ort a bhí an t-ádh nach bhfuil sé istigh.

AN BACACH: Tuige? Casadh fear bocht ar an mbóthar liom a thug cuntas breá dom air. Dúirt sé nach bhfaca sé a leithéide riamh.

MÁIRE: Deamhan focal bréige a dúirt an bacach sin. Ní fhaca mise a leithéid riamh ar chuma ar bith. Leis an fhírinne a insint bíonn sé amanta agus níl locht ar bith air, ach amanta eile b'fhearr duit gan a dhul níos gaire ná míle dó.

AN BACACH: Tá sé chomh drochmhúinte sin, an ea?

MÁIRE: Ní hé sin féin é; ach níl ag dul tríd a cheann ó mhaidin go hoíche ná ó Luan go Satharn, ach cíos, cíos, cíos! Agus duine ar bith nach mbeidh a chíos aige dó, go bhfóire Dia air!

AN BACACH: Muise agus go bhfóire Dia ormsa mar sin!

MÁIRE: Go deimhin, ba cheart dom a rá nach mbeadh sé leath chomh dona murach rógaire de bháille atá aige a bhíonn ag insint scéalta dó – tá faitíos orm mura ndíbreoidh sé é go mbeidh a cheann iompaithe aige, mura bhfuil ag Dia.

AN BACACH *(Ag corrú anonn agus anall)*: Cogar, ó tharla nach bhfuil sé féin ann, b'fhéidir go dtabharfá féin rud éigin do chréatúr bocht ar son Dé agus na Maighdine Muire.

MÁIRE: Cad tá ag teastáil uait ar chor ar bith?

AN BACACH: Airgead; píosa beag airgid - is é is deise agus is furasta a iompar.

MÁIRE: Ára, cá bhfaighinnse airgead, a mhic ó? Dá mbeadh sé agam gheofá é agus fáilte.

AN BACACH: B'fhéidir má dhéanann tú tóraíocht go bhfaighfeá é; déan agus go ndéana Dia trócaire ar anamna do mharbh!

MÁIRE: Deirim leat nach bhfuil pingin rua ná geal in mo sheilbh. B'fhéidir go bhfuil an oiread agat féin.

AN BACACH: An dáiríre atá tú? Créatúr bocht mar mise?

MÁIRE: Seo cúpla fata duit agus tabhair leat in do mhála iad agus déan airgead díobh.

AN BACACH: Go raibh maith agat agus fad saoil ach ní mórán áite atá agam dóibh anois. Déanfaidh píosa cáca agus braon bainne mé chomh maith, má tá siad agat; agus bog díom an mála seo, más é do thoil é. *(Tógann sí an mála óna dhroim).*

MÁIRE: Nach deacair tú a shásamh! Seo anois *(Ag tabhairt cáca agus bainne dó).* Ith agus ól suas iad seo go beo nó beidh sé féin isteach ar do mhullach.

AN BACACH: Déanfaidh sin. Cuirfidh mé dhá ghreim in aon ghreim amháin. Seo, cuir ruainne beag ime air seo, más é do thoil é.

MÁIRE: Go dtachta sé thú! Is mór an cleachtadh atá agat ar im go deimhin.

AN BACACH *(Leis féin):* Go bhféacha Dia orm! Is mairg a bheadh bocht! Bí ag tóraíocht seanbhríste dom anois chomh fada is atá mé ag ithe an bhéile seo – teastaíonn sé uaim go géar le haghaidh an gheimhridh.

MÁIRE: Cá bhfaighinnse bríste?

AN BACACH: Mura bhfuil sé agatsa b'fhéidir go bhfuil sé aige féin.

Tosaíonn Máire ag gáirí. Ólann an bacach an chuid is mó den bhainne, agus cuireann sé an chuid eile ins an gcanna stáin; cuireann sé fuílleach an aráin ins an mála beag, bán. Tá Máire taobh thiar de. Iompaíonn sé a dhroim, agus leagann sé a shúil uirthi, i ganfhios di, ag altú a bhéile go cráifeach!

AN BACACH: Bheirim mo bheannachtsa ag luí agus ag éirí duit; beannacht Mhuire agus a Mhic, na naomh agus na n-aingeal ort. Go méadaí Dia im agus bainne duit, agus go mba seacht míle fearr a bheas tú bliain ó inniu! Áiméan!

AN BACACH *(Leis féin tar éis breith ar an mála agus ag meá na bhfataí idir a dhá láimh):* M'anam go dtógfainn na fataí anois gur maith dom iad a fháil – is beag nach bhfuil trí clocha fataí anseo. *(Le Máire).* An bhfuil na fataí úd agat anois a bhí tú a bhronnadh orm tamall ó shin?

MÁIRE: Shíl mé nach raibh aon áit agat dóibh. Dheamhan ceann ba cheart a thabhairt duit anois, nuair nár thóg tú cheana iad.

AN BACACH: Shíl mé féin sin. Leis an fhírinne a inseacht, bhí mé go han-tuirseach agus bhí tart agus ocras orm, ach tá rud beag spreactha ionam anois, go lige Dia slán thusa. *(Croitheann sé é féin go teann agus go hard).* Tabhair dom iad má tá siad agat.

MÁIRE: Seo mar sin agus bí ag imeacht chomh tapaidh is atá sé in do chosa tú a iompar, nó má fheiceann sé féin thú brisfidh sé do chloigeann.

AN BACACH *(Go feargach):* Bhrisfeadh sé mo chloigeannsa, an ea? Bhí mé lá de mo shaol agus bhuailfinn lán a chraicinn air.

Féachann Máire air agus tosaíonn sí ag gáirí agus imíonn sí ar a gnó féin; féachann an bacach thart timpeall an tí chomh fada is atá sé ag fáisceadh na téide ar an mála agus leagann sé a shúil ar bhuidéal ar an mbord; téann sé anonn chuige.

AN BACACH: Cad é seo? *(Blaiseann sé di).* Ó, mo chraiceann ón diabhal gurb é an fuiscí poitín atá ann. Nach maith nach bhfaca mé é seo cheana! *(Ní fhágann sé deoir ins an mbuidéal; síneann sé é féin ar an gcathaoir, agus an bord taobh thiar de).* M'anam go mbeidh ceathrú breá amhráin anois agam.

Casann sé suas 'Contae Mhaigh Eo'; buaileann sé cúpla leadóg den mhaide ar an gcanna stáin. Nuair atá an t-amhrán leathráite aige tigeann Manders isteach).

MANDERS: Cén sórt diabhlaíochta atá ar bun anseo?

MÁIRE: Níl diabhlaíocht ar bith anseo ach an fear bocht seo a tháinig isteach tamall ó shin. Tá súil aige le rud éigin uaitse.

MANDERS: Agus cén fáth an gleo seo aige? Tuige ar lig tú

isteach ar chor ar bith é?

MÁIRE: Ní raibh sé mar sin nuair a tháinig sé isteach, pé bith a d'éirigh dó ó shin. Sílim anois go bhfuil sé ruidín beag éadrom ina chloigeann.

Féachann Manders idir an dá shúil ar an mbacach.

MANDERS *(Ag béicíl):* Cad tá tú a rá faoi bhacach? Nach é seo an gadaí atá ag siúl na tíre ag rá go bhfuil sé bacach agus gan bacaíocht air ach oiread agus atá ortsa nó ormsa? Ach ina dhiaidh sin, b'fhéidir go bhfuil mé ag déanamh éagóir ar an duine bocht. *(Téann sé isteach i ngar dó agus breathnaíonn sé anois air níos géire ná cheana; tigeann ballchrith ar Shéamas bocht le teann faitís).* Ó, go maithe Dia dom é! Tá agus éagóir mhór. *(Leis an mbacach).* Fan ansin, a dhuine bhoicht; tá ceirín thuas staighre agamsa agus b'fhéidir go leigheasfadh sé na scoilteacha sin atá 'do chreachadh.

Gabhann sé in airde.

AN BACACH *(Ag rith amach mar a rithfeadh giorria):* Coinnigh do sheancheirín agat féin, a Manders; b'fhéidir go dteastódh sé uait fós. *(Déanann sé dearmad ar an mála agus tagann sé isteach arís agus giorranáil air).* Cá bhfuil an mála – agus an bríste, an bhfuil sé agat? Ardaigh é seo orm go beo, más é do toil é. *(Ardaíonn sí an mála air).* Ní fheicim an bríste – cá bhfuil sé?

MÁIRE: Níl sé agam.

AN BACACH: Mura bhfuil, ná raibh sé agat. Slán leat anois. Is fada go bhfeicfidh tú mise arís, mo chailín. *(Ag bagairt an mhaide uirthi agus ag bualadh amach).*

Tig Manders anuas.

MANDERS: Cá bhfuil sé nó ar imigh sé amach?

MÁIRE: Tá tú as anois.

Ritheann Manders amach ina dhiaidh.

MANDERS *(Tar éis teacht ar ais)*: Siúd síos an bóthar é mar a bheadh giorria Márta ann, agus leathchéad meáchain ar a dhroim. Sin é an fear a dúirt tusa a bhí bacach. Bhí mé ag ceapadh i gcónaí gur leibide óinsí a bhí ionat ach anois tá mé lánchinnte gur ceann acu thú.

MÁIRE: Agus cén neart a bhí agamsa air? Tháinig sé isteach.

MANDERS: Éist do bhéal, a deirim leat. Shílfeadh duine ar bith gur teach ceoil a bhí agat ann – tú ag éisteacht leis an mbithiúnach gan pioc suime agat ann. *(Go feargach)*. Ach tá mé ag tabhairt comhairle duit anois, má dhéanann tú a leithéide arís, go rachaidh tú amach as an teach seo ar mhullach do chinn, agus bí in do leibide nó in d'óinsigh in áit éigin eile.

Téann Siobhán ar ais.

SIOBHÁN: Cad é seo, ar chor ar bith?

MANDERS: Duine uasal a bhí anseo romhainn a bhí ag ligint bacaíocht air féin agus a chuir an teach trína chéile leis an méid gleo a bhí ar bun aige agus gan blas suime ag Máire ann.

SIOBHÁN: Cé hé féin, ar chor ar bith?

MÁIRE: Dúirt sé gur de Mhuintir Phaoraigh é. As Bóithrín an tSliogáin é.

MANDERS: Muise, go bhfóire Dia ort! Dheamhan a fhios cén t-ainm atá air, mar nach é an t-ainm atá inniu air a bheas amárach air. Níor cheart di é a ligint isteach beag ná mór.

SIOBHÁN: Cad a d'fhéadfadh an créatúr a dhéanamh mura gcuirfeadh sí amach le maide é?

MANDERS: Bhí amhras agam ar dtús gurbh é Micheál Réidh a bhí ann. Nach fada atá Micheál gan teacht?

SIOBHÁN: Is túisce a ólfaidh tusa ná mise. Ach nach róluath a bheas sé ann, má bhíonn na trí cheist sin ar bharr a theangan aige duit?

MANDERS: Nach furasta leat na trí cheist sin a dhéanamh amach! Shíl mé féin go dtabharfadh sé a dhúshlán d'Aristotle na leabhar fadó iad siúd a dhéanamh amach.

SIOBHÁN: Agus má bhíonn na freagraí cearta aige nach gcaithfidh tú géilleadh dó?

MANDERS: Gan amhras.

Tig Conchúr isteach.

CONCHÚR: An raibh Micheál Réidh anseo ó shin?

MANDERS: Bhí, ach, má bhí féin, ba bheag an mhaith sin dúinne.

CONCHÚR: Agus cá bhfuil na páipéir mar sin?

MANDERS: Fan leat. Dúirt sé go raibh sé féin is a bhean is a chlann ina luí le sé seachtainí leis an slaghdán mór; go raibh muca aige agus go mb'éigean dó iad a dhíol le haghaidh purgóid agus dochtúir agus chuile shórt mar sin.

CONCHÚR: Agus ar chreid tú an cneamhaire sin tar éis an méid a d'inis mise duit?

MANDERS *(Go réidh):* Chreid agus níor chreid.

CONCHÚR: Ára, ná bí ag caitheamh do theanga leis an rógaire úd, ach tabhair dom na páipéir agus lig chun bealaigh mé.

MANDERS: Foighid ort. Cé a thiocfadh isteach an uair chéanna ach an bhean seo? D'iarr sí a phardún agus fuair sí é. Rinne mé athsmaoineamh ansin agus dúras le Micheál dá mbeadh sé in ann trí cheist a chuirfinn air a fhreagairt, ní hé amháin go maithfinn cíos na bliana seo dó ach go mbeadh a thalamh saor ó chíos arís go brách aige. *(Ag gealgháirí).* Ach, go deimhin, tá baol mór air go mbeidh sé in ann na ceisteanna a chuir mé air a réiteach!

CONCHÚR: B'fhéidir go bhfuil agus b'fhéidir nach bhfuil; ach mura bhfuil, gheobhaidh sé duine éigin a dhéanfas amach dó iad.

MANDERS: Agus cé hé an duine sin, le do thoil?

CONCHÚR: Tá sé ann; fear darbh ainm Seán Ó Murchú. Feicim in éineacht le Micheál go minic é. Dá siúlfá Éire agus Contae Mhaigh Eo ní bhfaighfeá aon bhithiúnach eile chomh mór le Seán Ó Murchú. Tá faitíos ar chuile dhuine roimhe, tá an oiread sin diabhlaíochta ina cheann. Níl sé trí lá ó mharaigh sé asal ar Thadhg Maoineach, an fear is cneasta sa bparóiste. Sin é an sórt comhluadair atá Micheál Réidh a choinneáil le tamall agus tá mé ag ceapadh freisin gurb é is ciontach gan an cíos a bheith ag Micheál inniu.

MANDERS: Is cuma liomsa cé is ciontach, ní bhrisfidh mise m'fhocal le fear ar bith. An bhfuil tú ag iarraidh na daoine mé a chaitheamh le gunna? An bhfaca tú na goithí a bhí ag Seán Páidín gabha ar ball?

CONCHÚR: Ná bíodh faitíos ar bith ort; tabhair scata breá saighdiúir leat, agus is beag an baol a bheas ort.

MANDERS: Go bhfóire Dia ort! Is iomaí fear a raibh saighdiúirí á ghardú cheana a fuair piléar ina dhiaidh sin a chuir deireadh lena shaol.

CONCHÚR: Is trua gan mise in d'áit, is beag an faitíos a bheadh ormsa.

Tig Seán isteach agus imíonn Conchúr amach. Tá culaith éadaigh Mhichíl ar Sheán agus é fá fhéasóig.

MANDERS: An bhfuil freagraí na dtrí cheist sin agat dom, a Mhichíl?

SEÁN: Dar fia, tá, a Mháisitr.

MANDERS: Amach leo, má tá. Anois cé mhéad meáchain atá ins an ngealaigh?

SEÁN: Tá ceithre ceathrúna.

MANDERS: Maith go leor. Anois cé mhéad réalt sa spéir?

SEÁN: Tá ocht milliún ceithre chéad déag go leith, chomh díreach agus atá eireaball ar chat.

MANDERS: Níl tú ceart. Tá níos mó ná sin ann.

SEÁN: Mura gcreide tú mise, amach leat thú féin agus comhairigh iad.

MANDERS *(Leis féin):* Dheamhan locht ar bith air. De réir cosúlachta, beidh an lá ag Seán. Cé hí an tríú ceist: cad tá mé a cheapadh in m'intinn?

SEÁN *(Tar éis smaoineamh):* Tá tú ag ceapadh go bhfuil tú ag caint le Micheál Réidh.

MANDERS: Agus nach bhfuilim?

SEÁN: Níl, a mh'anam! Tá tú ag caint le Seán Ó Murchú! *(Ag baint de na féasóige bréagaí).*

MANDERS: An ag caint le Seán Ó Murchú, an rógaire a mharaigh asal an Mhaoinigh an lá cheana atáim? *(Go feargach).* Bí ag imeacht as m'amharc agus ná feicim anseo níos mó thú.

Imíonn Seán go tapaidh.

SIOBHÁN: Sílim go bhfuil tú ag déanamh éagóir mhór ar Sheán Ó Murchú.

MANDERS: Nár mhionnaigh Conchúr gur mharaigh sé asal le Tadhg Maoineach?

SIOBHÁN: Ní chreidfinn é dá mionnódh sé ar Leabhar na hAltóra, mar chonaic mé an t-asal céanna a dúirt Conchúr a maraíodh ag dul trasna an tsrutháin inniu le ualach móna!

MANDERS: Glaoigh isteach ar Sheán Ó Murchú, a Mháire, agus abair leis go ndearna mé dearmad.

Tig Seán isteach arís.

MANDERS: An tusa Seán Ó Murchú?

SEÁN: Is mé go cinnte.

MANDERS: An bhfuil fear eile sa bparóiste darb ainm Séamas Ó Murchú?

SEÁN: Tá, a mháistir.

MANDERS: Sin é a bhí in m'aigne nuair a chuala mé an sloinne 'Ó Murchú'. Seo anois píosa corónach duit mar gheall ar an ngeit a bhain mé asat; agus nuair a bheas tú amuigh abair le Micheál – Micheál, ceart – a theacht isteach – go bhfuil gnó beag agam de.

SEÁN *(Leis féin, ag dul amach):* Níl an diabhal chomh dona agus atá a cháil.

Tig Micheál isteach.

MANDERS: Ghnóthaigh tú an cluiche sin, a Mhichíl.

MICHEÁL: Bím buíoch de Sheán Ó Murchú ar a shon sin.

MANDERS: Ní bhrisfidh mise m'fhocal leat. Seo anois admháil duit faoi mo láimh inniu go mbeidh do thalamh gan cíos gan cáin agat agus ag do shliocht 'do dhiaidh, chomh fada agus a bheas uisce ag rith nó féar ag fás!

MICHEÁL: Go raibh míle maith agat agus fad saoil agat, a mháistir, agus ag do chéile chaoin, charthanaigh ar son do mhórmhaitheas domsa anocht. Ó, míle moladh agus altú le Dia, nach orm a bhí an t-ádh ag éirí dom ar maidin!

MANDERS: Is féidir leatsa dul amach anois, a Mhichíl, tá do chúis réitithe, agus abair le Conchúr agus leis na tionóntaí eile teacht anseo.

Tig siad isteach.

MANDERS *(Le Conchúr):* A Chonchúir, tá tú fiche bliain in mo sheirbhís anois, agus bhí tuairim agam i gcónaí gur fear fírinneach, cneasta a bhí ionat ach feicim anois go raibh mé ag dul amú go mór. Tuige a ndúirt tú gur mharaigh Seán Ó Murchú asal an Mhaoinigh?

CONCHÚR: Níor dhúirt mise ach an rud a chuala mé féin. Más bréag é ní mise a chum é.

MANDERS: Dún do bhéal! Nach tú a bhí simplí! Is mór an t-ionadh liomsa nár chreid tú iad bliain ó shin nuair a dúirt siad gur tú féin a ghearr scornach an tseanchapaill chramptha a bhí agat, agus a chuir do scioból faoi lasadh, ag súil go mbainfeá spaigín bheag airgid as muintir an chontae, ach i leaba airgid is é an príosún a gheofá murach gur labhair mise ar do shon.

CONCHÚR: Is mór an t-ionadh liomsa go gcreidfeá na daoine úd tar éis chomh fada agus atá mé in do sheirbhís.

MANDERS: Há! Há! Bhí tú in d'fhear bhocht nuair a ghlac mé thú in mo sheirbhís ar dtús. Ní raibh agat an t-am sin ach seanasal bacach agus dhá ghabhar. Anois níl fear ar mo dhúthaigh chomh saibhir leat. Ó, beidh an smaoineamh ag ithe agus ag creimeadh mo chroí agus mo choinsias, chomh fada agus a mhairfeas mé, go dtug mé aird ar do dhroch-chomhairle go minic, mar is iomaí tine a mhúch mé, agus is iomaí muirín a scaip mé mar gheall uirthi. Agus an lá a chuir mé amach iad scaip siad ó chéile – an t-athair ón mac agus an iníon ón máthair, b'fhéidir gan teacht le chéile arís go brách go dtí Lá an Bhreithiúnais. Fuair cuid eile acu bás le anó agus briseadh croí agus fuair siad foscadh agus dídean san uaigh, mar bhí sí níos carthanaí ná mise. Bhí mé ag brath ar na gabháltais a fuair tú uaim le fealltóireacht agus le gliceas a bhaint díot, agus na daoine a dhíbir mé astu a chur ar ais orthu arís; ach ar athsmaoineamh, coinnigh iad, mar nach bhfuil formhór na ndaoine le fáil anois – ach an méid atá ar fáil, tabharfaidh mise gabháltais níos fearr dóibh. Cuirfidh mise na daoine seo as do chumhacht, agus as cumhacht do leithéide arís go brách.

CONCHÚR: Go raibh maith agat; murach mise b'fhéidir gur lú ná sin a bheadh agat féin.

MANDERS: Imigh leat anois, a bhuachaill. Ní bheidh do sheirbhís ag teastáil uaimse níos mó.

Imíonn sé amach. Dúnann na tionóntaí an doras ina dhiaidh.

MANDERS: Ó tharla go bhfuair mé amach gur mealladh mé le bréagadóireacht agus saobhchaint Chonchúir déanfaidh mé anois an oiread cúitimh agus atá sé in mo chumas. Bhí mé ag smaoineamh in m'aigne le tamall go bhfuil sé in am ag Tiarnaí Talún na tíre seo iarracht éigin a dhéanamh le cosc a chur leis na daoine a bheith ag fágáil na tíre ina mílte mar atá siad. Ar an ábhar sin, tá fíor-rún agam féin páirt fir a dhéanamh agus mo chuid tionóntaí féin a choinneáil ins an mbaile má fhéadaim. Sílim nach bhfuil aon chaoi níos fearr leis sin a dhéanamh ná an talamh atá in mo sheilbh féin a roinnt amach agus bhur bhfeilmne a mhéadú ionas go mbeidh sibh in ann maireachtáil go compordúil orthu; is ansin iad a dhíol amach libh go brách ar chíos fiche bliain; agus cíos ar bith atá amuigh oraibh, maithfidh mé daoibh é. An mbeidh sibh sásta leis sin?

DIARMAID Ó MÁILLE: Táimid buíoch díot, a mháistir, ar son an tsocraithe seo atá tú a dhéanamh linn; ach tá a fhios agat san am céanna gur sinn féin agus ár n-aithreacha romhainn a rinne talamh di; níl fál ná claí nár thógamar ná leachtán cloiche nár thochlaíomar amach; ar an ábhar sin bhíomar ag ceapadh go mbeifeá sásta le cíos sé bliana déag.

SIOBHÁN: An méid atá eadraibh, scoiltigí é; is é sin ceannaítear agus díoltar an talamh ar chíos ocht mbliana déag.

DIARMAID Ó MÁILLE: Is fear bocht mise agus ní bhrisfinn focal mná uaisle ar chúig phunt.

IAD UILE: Ná muidne.

MANDERS: Ná mise ach an oiread – bíodh sé mar sin. Anois beidh an chúis seo réitithe ins an gcúirt i gceann míosa nó mar sin agus ón lá sin amach ní chuirfidh an báille, fear na bpróiseannna, ná an reithe réabtha aon trioblóid oraibh níos mó!

BRAT

An Deoraí

Dráma in aghaidh imeacht thar sáile

An Fhoireann

Peadar Ó Ceallaigh, fear an tí

Maighréad Uí Cheallaigh, a bhean

Cáit Ní Cheallaigh, a iníon atá ag brath ar imeacht go Meiriceá

Máirtín Ó Roighin, atá i ngrá le Cáit

Eibhlín Ní Roighin, deirfiúr Mháirtín

Marcas Ó Conghaile, fear ar thóir mná

Máire Ní Eidhin, bean tar éis filleadh ó Mheiriceá

Micheál Mac Suibhne
Stiofán Bacach – comharsanaigh
Michilín Crosach, Údarás an Bhaile
Siobhán Ní Ghuimhiullaidh

Píobaire agus daoine eile

Áit: Cisteanach i dtigh feilméara in Éirinn
An t-am: Faoi láthair

Tá Cáit ag socrú bosca le haghaidh dul go Meiriceá; nuair atá sí ag brath ar é a dhúnadh agus an glas a chur air, tig Maighréad isteach.

MAIGHRÉAD: Mura dtóga tú na stocaí seo, cuir an glas ar an mbosca sin go beo, nó má fheiceann d'athair an t-éadach gallda atá thíos ann, dófaidh sé sa tine iad.

CÁIT: Déanfaidh Nóra atá i Meiriceá an cleas céanna leis na stocaí atá in do láimh agat. Tá tú ag iarraidh ormsa a dtabhairt liom in aghaidh mo thola.

MAIGHRÉAD: Mar gheall air gur in Éirinn a rinneadh iad, an ea?

CÁIT: Creidim gurb ea. Nach bhfaca tú nuair a bhí sí sa mbaile nach siúlfadh sí coiscéim den bhóthar liom dá bhfeicfeadh sí mé ag caitheamh éadaí ar bith ach an cineál a thiocfadh anall thar sáile chugainn?

MAIGHRÉAD: Is mór a d'athraigh an saol ó shin, a Cháit. Tá áiteacha i Meiriceá féin faoi láthair ann a bhfuil meas mór ar theanga na hÉireann is meas dá réir ar dhéantúis na hÉireann.

CÁIT: B'fhéidir sin ach má tá Nóra ins an fhaisean gallda, nach gcaithfidh mise a sampla a leanúint ó tharla gurbh í a chuir fios orm?

MAIGHRÉAD: Faraor, lig mé cead do chinn leat ó rugadh thú is ní fiú gan é a thabhairt duit anois nuair atá tú ag imeacht uaim.

CÁIT: Le ómós duitse, béarfaidh mé liom iad – ó tharla go bhfuil mé ag imeacht, ní mórán ualaigh orm iad ar chuma ar bith.

Cuireann Maighréad na stocaí sa mbosca. Tig Peadar, fear an tí, isteach tar éis é a bheith ag Aonach Bhaile i bhFad Siar.

PEADAR: A Cháit, a stór, an bhfuil tú ag imeacht uaim chomh luath sin? Níor shíl mé go rachfá go Meiriceá go dtagadh an chéad soitheach eile isteach i gceann coicíse. Ní raibh cosúlacht imeachta ar chor ar bith ort ar maidin. Dar ndóigh, ní féidir gur chuir na cúpla focal úd a dúirt mé leat i dtaobh an chleamhnais bhig a bhí mé ag iarraidh a dhéanamh idir sinn féin agus Marcas Ó Conghaile aon fhearg ort.

CÁIT: Go deimhin, níor chuir, a athair. Ach fuair mé scéal ó d'imigh tú go mbeadh an long ag fágáil Chuan Chorcaí arú amárach. Creidim dá bhfanfainn níos faide ins an tír bhocht, uaigneach seo go mbrisfí mo chroí. Is fada liom go mbeidh mé thall i Meiriceá an áit a mbeidh rud éigin de bharr mo shaothair agam – rud nach mbeadh anseo dá bhfanfainn ann go brách.

PEADAR: Á, a Cháit, bhí tú ag déanamh maith go leor sa mbaile dá mbeadh ciall agat. Is iomaí cailín a bheadh ríméadach a dó dhéag is sé pingine sa tseachtain a fháil le saothrú. Bhí tusa ag fáil an mhéid sin gan mórán trioblóide – ag déanamh lása faoin mBord Ceardúil, gan call agat do lámha a shalú ó mhaidin go hoíche.

CÁIT: Ára, a dhaide, níl in dó dhéag is sé pingine ach pá mugadh magadh – nach saothróinn é sin in aon lá amháin i Meiriceá? Shaothróinn a thrí oiread sa tseachtain ar a laghad.

PEADAR: Agus cuir i gcás go saothrófá a thrí oiread sa tseachtain, nuair a bhainfeá do lóistín agus do bheathú as sin, cad a bheadh agat?

CÁIT: Dá bhfaighinn a sheacht n-oiread déag sa tseachtain níl goir agam fanacht sa mbaile. Nach bhfaca tú an litir a chuir Nóra chugam tá coicís ó shin? Dúirt sí nach mbeadh sí beo mura dtéinn anonn chuici.

MAIGHRÉAD: Agus cén fáth é sin?

CÁIT: Bheadh an oiread sin cumha uirthi, deir sí.

PEADAR: Nach aisteach an rud é sin agus an méid cailíní beaga atá as an áit seo in éineacht léi.

CÁIT: Níl duine ar bith as an áit seo in éineacht léi anois mar d'athraigh sí as an mbaile mór a raibh sí ann.

PEADAR: Mise i mbannaí gur athraigh. B'fhéidir go mb'fhearr di fanacht san áit a raibh sí dá dhonacht é.

CÁIT: Dá dhonacht é! Seo litir eile a fuair mé ó Nóra inniu. Fosclóidh sé do shúile duit i dtaobh an tsaibhris agus an tsaoil bhreá atá aici féin agus ag na daoine a chuaigh go Meiriceá as an gceantar seo le cúpla bliain.

PEADAR: Bhí mé ag ceapadh go bhfuair tú rud éigin a bhí do do dheifriú thar sáile; ach tá amhras mór orm gur ceann de na litreacha bréagacha seo í atá ag déanamh an oiread sin díobhála ar mhuintir na tíre seo. Léigh amach go beo í go bhfeicimid cad tá ann!

CÁIT (*Ag léamh na litreach*): 'A Cháit, mo chroí thú,' ar sise, 'ná géill d'éinne a chuireas comhairle ort fanacht sa mbaile. Go bhfóire Dia ort! Cad tá tú ach id sclábhaí bhocht in Éirinn. Beidh tú id mhnaoi uasal i Meiriceá. Féach mise! Ní thiocfainn ar ais go hÉirinn anois dá bhfaighinn airgead Rí Sheoirse. Tá brat urláir breá galánta faoi mo chosa ó éirím ar maidin go dtéim 'mo chodladh san oíche. Níl fútsa ó mhaidin go hoíche ach salachar na mbóithre brocacha. Maidir le ór is airgead, tá siad anseo chomh fairsing le sprémhóin sa mbaile. Chuala mé fear eolasach á rá an lá cheana atá in ann airgead a chomhaireamh chomh maith le Pitagóras na bhFigiúirí fadó, go bhfuil faoi dhó an oiread airgid i Meiriceá agus atá siad in ann úsáid a dhéanamh de agus, de réir mar atá sé ag méadú ann, a deir sé, feicfir an tír seo fós agus ní bheidh aon mheas ar airgead ann ach an oiread agus atá ar chlocha beaga in Éirinn.'

PEADAR: Agus má tá sé chomh fairsing sin ann, a Cháit, nach sinn na hamadáin nach dtéann anonn agus corrmhála a thabhairt anall anseo agus chomh géar agus atá sé ag teastáil! Ach tiomáin leat.

CÁIT (*Ag léamh*): 'Ní bréag nach bhfuil na comharsanaigh ag déanamh go han-mhaith ins an tír álainn seo. Ar ndóigh, bhí aithne agat ar Mháire Ní Eidhin a d'imigh as Cnoc an tSeanbhaile fadó. Ní aithneofá anois í thar bhean Uachtarán Mheiriceá le saibhreas agus mórgacht an tsaoil. Níl call uirthi a bróga a shalú ag dul trasna na sráide mar tá cóiste agus ceithre chapall ullmhaithe lena hiompar chuile áit den bhaile mhór is mian léi dul ann. Tá searbhóntaí agus buitléirí aici as éadan a chéile agus ní hé an gléas céanna a chuirfidh sí uirthi féin anois a bheidh uirthi ar ball. Tá slabhra mór buí faoina muineál a cheanglódh bád Mhichíl Thaidhg, agus tá péire bróg aici á chaitheamh a chosain cúig *dollar* go leith ina bhfuil na sála atá orthu leath-throigh ar airde, agus na bonnachaí chomh tanaí le píosa trí pingine! Is cumasach an tír í le haghaidh fir amach is amach! Tá Máirtín Ó Ciaráin – grabaire beag a d'imigh as Baile na mBroc cúpla bliain ó shin – ag saothrú ocht *dollar* sa ló ina stiúrthóir ar bhóthar iarainn agus an oiread fear faoina chúram go dtógfadh sé lá is bliain le hiad a chomhaireamh. Nuair a bhí Máirtín sa mbaile ag gabháil bata ar an seanasal ní raibh bróg faoina chois; anois tá uaireadóir ina phóca aige a chosain céad go leith *dollar*, agus slabhraí móra buí á choinneáil chomh ramhar le súgán a d'fheicfeá thart timpeall coca féir. Ach, le críoch a chur leis an litir seo, más mian leat a bheith id sclábhaí ag a leithéide seo agus ag a leithéide siúd, fan sa mbaile; ach más áil leat a bheith ar rothaí an tsaoil, tar anall anseo.'

PEADAR: An é sin an méid bréag atá ann?

CÁIT: Níor inis sí leath na fírinne ann.

MAIGHRÉAD: Is cosúil leis an bhfírinne í ar chuma ar bith.

PEADAR: Is cosúil go deimhin! An áit a bhfeileann an fhírinne, instear an fhírinne, ach an áit nach bhfeileann, instear an bhréag go minic.

MAIGHRÉAD: Dá mba aingeal as an bhflaitheas a d'inseodh duitse é, ní chreidfeá é.

PEADAR: Éist do bhéal, a deirim leat, nó fágfaidh mé an teach. Nach simplí a cheapann tú na daoine a bheith. (*Ag smaoineamh*). Ach ar uacht an tsicín sháraigh scéal Mháirtín Uí Chiaráin an méid a chualas riamh nó a chloisfidh mé go brách. M'anam gurbh é Máirtín a chonaic a dhá shaol ach ní mór liomsa dó é, an duine bocht!

MAIGHRÉAD: Ní mór, ná liomsa, ach má tá leath an mhéid sin aige, ba cheart dó cuimhneamh ar a mháthair bhocht a bheadh caillte le hanó le ráithe murach chomh ceanúil agus atá na comharsanaigh uirthi.

CÁIT: B'fhéidir gur á ól atá an bithiúnach.

PEADAR: Ná bígí chomh dian sin ar an duine bocht tar éis an méid cáile atá ar Mháirtín. B'fhéidir nach bhfuil an oiread aige agus a d'íocfadh a bhealach abhaile, ach, má tá, 'is maith an scéalaí an aimsir.'

CÁIT: Tá mise ag dul amach anois, a mhama, go bhfága mé slán ag Peigse Bhríd Mhóir. Tá sí chomh buailte suas sin leis na scoilteacha nach bhfuil sí in ann teacht anseo anocht.

MAIGHRÉAD: Go ngnóthaí Dia duit, a stór.

Imíonn Cáit amach.

PEADAR: Is cosúil, a Mhaighréad, nach bhfuil aon mhaith a bheith ag iarraidh ortsa comhairle a chur ar Cháit. Caithfidh sí dul anonn go Meiriceá le í a bheith ina mnaoi uasal?

MAIGHRÉAD: Ní abróidh mise sea nó ní hea – déanadh sí an rud is mian léi.

PEADAR: Déanadh sí an rud is mian léi, an ea! Is minic a dúirt tú é sin ó d'fhág sí an cliabhán; is beag an dochar í a bheith ina peata agat.

MAIGHRÉAD: Má tá sí ina peata, ní mise a rinne peata di. Ní mé a rinne peata de Sheán nuair a d'imigh sé, a cheann roimhe, ar uair an mheán oíche tar éis fiche punt a ghoid uait, gan an oiread agus a bheannacht a fhágáil ag na comharsanaigh.

PEADAR: Muise, go n-éirí sé leis an duine bocht – sin é a bhfuil le rá agamsa. Pé bith rud a thug sé leis, is é féin a shaothraigh go crua é, agus ba mhaith uaidh é a shaothrú.

MAIGHRÉAD: Ní hí sin an phaidir a bhí agat dó nuair a d'airigh tú imithe é.

PEADAR: Mar bhí rud beag feirge orm an uair sin agus níor chuimhnigh mé orm féin i gceart. Ach an measann tú an gcuirfidh fiche punt i mbeala (sic!) an 'Éirí Amach' nó an *Rendezvous* a bheas anseo ar ball? Is beag an baol. Tá faitíos orm go gcuirfidh sé as an teach sinn mura bhfuil ag Dia.

Ag caitheamh na cathaoireach uaidh le teann taighd.

MAIGHRÉAD: Ní chuirfidh, le cúnamh Dé – nach é lá dár saol é! Anois, ar son Dé, lig amach an cailín beag go gnaíúil agus ná bíodh an tír ag magadh fúinn amárach.

PEADAR: An tír ag magadh fúinn, an ea! Muise, ar ndóigh, níl aon tír sa domhan nach bhfuil ag magadh fúinn cheana; níl ann anois ach 'cáide go mbeidh tú ag dul go Meiriceá, a Phádraig, nó, a Bhríd? Ára, cá mbeifeá ag fanacht? Beidh oíche bhreá againn ort.' Seo í an chomhairle atá an t-aos óg a fháil anois chomh luath agus atá siad in ann cótaí beaga a chaitheamh.

MAIGHRÉAD: Anois cén mhaith duit a bheith ag caismirt mar sin, ach cuir fios ar na comharsanaigh nach bhfuair cuireadh cheana.

PEADAR (*Go feargach*): Cuir fios ar an tír más breá leat é; ach deirimse leatsa gur beag an fháilte a bheas agamsa roimh a leath!

Tig Cáit isteach agus culaith éadaigh Mheiriceá uirthi.

CÁIT: Thug mise cuireadh dóibh ar fad ach do Mharcas Ó Conghaile.

PEADAR: Agus, má thug tú cuireadh dóibh ar fad, tuige ar fhág tú Marcas 'do dhiaidh?

MAIGHRÉAD: Muise, bhí mé ag ceapadh go dtiocfadh sé gan cuireadh ar bith mar nach raibh sé riamh ar deireadh.

PEADAR: Is cuma sin. Is é an chéad fhear a gcuirfinnse fios air.

MAIGHRÉAD: Nach cúramach atá tú faoi, go deimhin. Is beag an brabach a gheofá ag a theach féin.

PEADAR: Is beag! Nuair a bhí cúnamh ag teastáil uainne anuraidh, thug sé dúinne é nuair a d'fhan do dheartháir sa mbaile ag tabhairt aire dá ghnó féin.

MAIGHRÉAD: Ní ar mhaithe leatsa ná liomsa a tháinig Marcas ach ar mhaithe leis féin.

PEADAR: Go díreach! 'Ar mhaithe leis féin a dhéanas an cat crónán.' Murach é ina dhiaidh sin nach mbeadh do dhíol caite anuraidh? Ní bheadh fata le n-ithe agat – bheidís dóite ag an sioc.

MAIGHRÉAD: Sílim gur mó a d'ith sé ná a bhain sé.

PEADAR: Ní fhéadfadh sé a ithe ach a dhóthain. Ní bheidh níos mó ina thimpeall. Rachad ina choinne mé féin.

Imíonn sé.

MAIGHRÉAD (*Ag gol*): Tá tú ag imeacht anocht, a Cháit, agus is é an cás céanna domsa tú a chur go Meiriceá agus tú a chur san uaigh.

CÁIT: A mháthair, mo chroí thú, ná habair é sin! Dá dtéinn san uaigh ní fheicfeá choíche mé. B'fhéidir go gcuirfinn fios oraibh go léir fós.

MAIGHRÉAD: Grá mo chroí thú, a stóirín. (*Pógann sí Cáit*). Cuir fios orainn má bheidh sé in do chumas mar is beag é sólás mo shaoilse 'do dhiaidh.

CÁIT: Más mian leat, a mhama, cuirfidh mé mo phictiúr chugat le féachaint air anois agus arís.

MAIGHRÉAD: Seol chugainn é ins an gcéad litir a chuirfidh tú anall agus [gach] uile litir eile a chuirfeas tú chugainn, cuir rud éigin an taobh istigh di i dtreo nach mbeidh sé le rá agam le duine ar bith gur chuir tú litir fholamh abhaile.

CÁIT: Go deimhin, a mhama, ní chuirfidh mé aon litir fholamh abhaile má fhéadaim.

PEADAR (*Ag teacht isteach*): Má chuireann féin, a Cháit, beidh fáilte agus fiche rompu gí gur in aghaidh mo thola atá tú ag dul ann ar chor ar bith.

MAIGHRÉAD: Shíl mé go raibh tú leath bealaigh ó shin, a Pheadair.

PEADAR: Go deimhin, ní raibh call agam cos a chorraí ón gcos eile mar tá Marcas ag teacht aníos an bóthar chomh sciobtha le capall rása.

MAIGHRÉAD: Sea anois, ní chreidfeá mise.

Imíonn Cáit.

PEADAR: Bí deas, lách le Marcas anois, a Mhaighréad. Dheamhan blas dochair sa gcréatúr ach go mbíonn a theanga ruidín beag rófhada mar a bhíos ár dteangacha féin go minic.

MAIGHRÉAD (*Ar leataobh*): Is beag an beann atá agamsa air, é féin nó ar a theanga.

Tig Marcas isteach agus giorranáil air.

MARCAS: Bail ó Dhia agus ó Mhuire oraibh!

PEADAR: Go maire tú, a Mharcais. Cén chaoi a bhfuil do cheithre cnámha?

MARCAS: Cén mhaith a bheith ag casaoid, a Pheadair? (*Féachann sé thart timpeall air go huafásach*). Ní fheicim fear strainséartha ar bith anseo ach mé féin. Ní féidir gur imithe atá Cáit go bhfaighinn aon amharc amháin uirthi. Bhí mo shuipéar réidh ar an mbord ag fágáil an tí dom agus níor lig an deifir dom blaiseadh de le faitíos go mbeadh sí imithe romham.

MAIGHRÉAD (*Ar leataobh*): Ní raibh ag cur imní ort riamh ach do sheanbholg agus ní bheidh go brách.

MARCAS: Tá mé chomh brónach ina diaidh is dá mba í mo dheirfiúr a bheadh ann.

Glaonn Peadar ar Cháit agus tagann sí aniar as an tseomra.

CÁIT: Céad míle fáilte romhat, a Mharcais.

MARCAS: Tá tú ag imeacht uainn anocht, a Cháit, agus go n-éirí an t-ádh leat cibé cearn den domhan a shroichfeas tú. Agus éireoidh, le cúnamh Dé, mar tá beannacht na gcomharsanach go léir agat agus bhí ó bhí tú 'do leanbh. Ní dheachaigh aon chailín beag go Meiriceá le fiche bliain a bhfuil an oiread caithimh ina diaidh agam agus atá in do dhiaidhse.

CÁIT: Go raibh míle maith agat agus fad saoil agat, a Mharcais! Cuirfidh mise rolla tobac is píopa breá, galánta abhaile chugat.

MARCAS: Agus cuirfidh mise mo bheannacht chugatsa, a Cháit.

Tig Máirtín Ó Roighin, Eibhlín Ní Roighin is Micheál Mac Suibhne isteach. Téann Peadar ag cogarnach le Máirtín agus taispeánann sé Marcas dó.

MÁIRTÍN: Hó, hó! Tá tusa anseo freisin – nach luath a tháinig tú, a Mharcais?

MARCAS: Nach mór ort é, a Mháirtín! An gcuala tú riamh é, bíonn an t-ádh i ndiaidh na tráthúlachta?

MÁIRTÍN: Bíonn, agus i ndiaidh na simplíochta, a Mharcais. Go deimhin, ní mór liomsa duit buntáiste ar bith a gheobhas tú; ach ní maith liom duine ag teacht anseo anocht (is) a dhá láimh chomh fada le chéile.

MARCAS: Ní thuigim thú, a Mháirtín.

MÁIRTÍN (*Ag féachaint go crua ar Mharcas):* Cá bhfuil an bronntanas a thug tú leat?

MARCAS: Cé lena aghaidh an bronntanas, a Mháirtín?

MÁIRTÍN: Le haghaidh an chailín óig atá ag imeacht go Meiriceá. Nach bhfuil a fhios agat go maith nach ndeachaigh aon chailín óg go Meiriceá as an gceantar seo le fiche bliain nach bhfaigheadh sí rud éigin ó na comharsanaigh?

MICHEÁL MAC SUIBHNE: Is fíor duit, a Mháirtín. Ní dheachaigh aon chailín go Meiriceá riamh nach bhfaigheadh sí rud éigin ag imeacht di.

MÁIRTÍN: Anois, a Mharcais.

MARCAS: Agus cá bhfuil do bhronntanas féin, a Mháirtín? Ní fheicim tada agat ach an oiread liomsa.

MÁIRTÍN: Nach cuma duit?

MARCAS: Ní cuma liom. Dá dtéadh sé go dtí sin, nach mó mo ghaol féin leis an teach seo ná do ghaolsa?

MÁIRTÍN: Ó, foighid ort, a mhic ó! Cogar, a Mhaighréad.

MAIGHRÉAD: Sea, a Mháirtín.

MÁIRTÍN: Cé againn is mó gaol leis an teach seo – mise nó Marcas?

MAIGHRÉAD: Tusa gan amhras.

MARCAS: Ó, gabhaim pardún agaibh. Ó tharla go bhfuil iachall orm bronntanas a thabhairt uaim, cén sórt bronntanais a thabharfas mé liom?

MÁIRTÍN: Rud ar bith is breá leat.

MARCAS (*Ag imeacht amach*): Rud ar bith is breá liom. Déanfaidh sin.

MÁIRTÍN (*Go brónach le Cáit*): Muise, a Cháit mo chroí thú! Níor shíl mé go dtiocfadh an lá seo choíche go mbeadh iachall orm bronntanas a thabhairt duit agus tú ag imeacht go Meiriceá uaim.

Tarraingíonn sé hata agus cúpla úll aníos as bosca beag agus tabharann sé do Cháit iad is gabhann sí buíochas.

CÁIT: Á, a Mháirtín, ní mar a shíltear a bhítear. Ach croch thú féin suas. B'fhéidir go gcuirfinn fios ort i gceann bliana nó mar sin.

MÁIRTÍN: M'anam, má chuireann, a Cháit, go mbeidh mise agat gan mórán moille.

Tig Siobhán Ní Ghuimhiullaidh (comharsa) isteach.

SIOBHÁN: Go mbeannaí Dia anseo!

CÁIT: Go mbeannaí Dia is Muire duit, a Shiobhán.

SIOBHÁN: A Cháit, a mhuirnín, cad a dhéanfaidh mé ar chor ar bith nuair a bheas tú imithe uaim?

CÁIT: Nach mbeidh mise chomh brónach 'do dhiaidhse, a Shiobhán?

SIOBHÁN: Seo naipcín a cheannaigh mo mhama inniu duit. Coinneoidh sé go breá te thú ag dul anonn.

Gabhann Cáit buíochas agus cuireann sí an naipcín uirthi féin.

MÁIRTÍN: Muise, go maire tú is go gcaithe tú é, a Cháit, agus céad ceann is fearr ná é. Ní náire don chailín óg a thug duit é. Is cosúil é leis an gceann a fuair Bríd Bheag ag dul anonn go California tá coicís ó shin.

Tig Bríd Ní Dhraighneáin isteach agus cáca mine coirce i bpáipéar ina láimh aici.

BRÍD: A Cháit, mo chroí thú. Ní bheidh comrádaí ar bith agam anois nuair a bheas tusa imithe.

CÁIT: Labharfad le hÚna Mhór agus cuirfidh mé iachall uirthi fios a chur ort má fhéadaim. Cad é seo atá agat, a Bhríd?

BRÍD: Cáca mine coirce atá ann duitse. Deirtear gur breá é in aghaidh tinneas farraige agus, má bheidh aon fhuílleach ann, tabharfaidh tú ruainne bheag do Mháire Phaits Bháin agus cuir an chuid eile faoi do philiúr ionas go mbeidh tú ag brionglóid orainn ar fad.

CÁIT: Go raibh maith agus fad saoil agat, a Bhríd. Ach, féach, bhí a fhios agam nach mbeadh Stiofán ar deireadh.

Tig Stiofán Bacach isteach agus maide mór draighin ina lámh aige.

STIOFÁN: Bail ó Dhia anseo isteach. Agus tá Cáit ag imeacht faoi dheireadh. Seo, a Cháit, an maide draighin seo duit, agus tabhair do Pheadar Bhríd Shama é atá thall san áit a bhfuil Peig. Cuirfidh sé i gcuimhne dó an léasadh breá a thug a athair dó an lá fadó a d'fhan sé sa mbaile ón scoil ag baint airní liomsa ins an mball céanna ar fhás an maide seo ann. Níl aon ní eile agam le tabhairt dó ach mo bheannacht.

CÁIT: Déanfaidh sin. Bhéarfaidh mise dó iad is fáilte.

Tig Marcas isteach is fód móna faoina ascaill aige.

MÁIRTÍN: Ní raibh tú i bhfad ó shin, a Mharcais. Cad é seo atá agat? Fód móna ar m'anam. Airiú, an as do chiall atá tú? Nó an ag iarraidh a bheith ag magadh faoi na daoine a tháinig tú anseo anocht? Téann sé tríom dhá leith a dhéanamh de ar do sheanchloigeann cranda.

MARCAS: Hu, hu! Tóg comhairle do leasa, a mhic ó. Ná déan faice tráthnóna a mbeidh aiféala ort faoi ar maidin. Nár dhúirt tú rud ar bith is breá liom a thabhairt liom?

MÁIRTÍN: Má dúras, níor dhúirt mé leat fód móna a thabhairt do chailín gnaíúil. Go deimhin, dá shuaraí thú, níor shíl mé go ndéanfá rud chomh tuatach sin.

MARCAS: Ní mise an chéad fhear riamh a thug fód móna do dhuine a bheadh ag dul go Meiriceá. (*Le Micheál Mac Suibhne*). Ar ndóigh, ní mé, a Mhichíl? Is fear eolasach thú ar ghnása na tíre seo.

MICHEÁL MAC SUIBHNE: Go deimhin, ní tú, a Mharcais.

MARCAS: Agus nach iomaí file mar tú féin (slán an comhartha!) a chum scéal nó amhrán i dtaobh rud níos lú ná fód móna?

MICHEÁL: Is iomaí go cinnte, a Mharcais, is is iomaí deoraí bocht as Éirinn ar bhain fód móna mar é sin deora as a shúil.

CÁIT: Tá mise chomh buíoch díot, a Mharcais, is dá dtabharfá an portach ar fad dom.

MARCAS: An gcuala tú sin, a Mháirtín? Tá sí chomh buíoch díom anois is dá ndúnfá do bhéal.

MÁIRTÍN: Déanfaidh sin, a Cháit. Má tá tusa sásta leis an tairgsin úd, tá mise sásta leis.

MARCAS: Seo anois, a Cháit, a stór, ó tharla gur thóg tú an fód móna uaim, tóg an cláirín seo freisin is tabhair do mo dheartháir é atá thall i San Louis. Scríobh sé chugam an lá cheana is dúirt sé liom é a chur chuige chomh luath agus a d'fhéadfainn. Céad slán dó! Is iomaí fód móna a d'iompair sé leis an gcláirín sin riamh.

MÁIRTÍN: Muise, nár stopa tú go dtabharfaidh tú an portach ar do chruit leat.

Tig Michilín isteach is leaba chlúimh ar a dhroim aige.

MICHILÍN: Ó, go mbeannaí Dia isteach anseo. Cén chaoi a bhfuil chuile dhuine agaibh? Tá tú ag imeacht, a Cháit, is ba mhór an scéal é. Seo leaba bhreá chlúimh duit – déanfaidh sé thú go breá compordach ag dul anonn.

Clúmh géabha é sin ar fad cé is moite de chlúmh aon ghandail amháin. Abróidh tú le Billiuch nuair a rachaidh tú anonn go bhfuil clúmh an ghandail mhóir ansin a bhíodh ag baint greamanna as a cholpaí fada ó shin nuair a bhíodh sé ag seoladh na mbeithíoch.

MÁIRTÍN (*Ag féachaint ar an leaba chlúimh*): Nach deas iad na bronntanais atá tú a fháil, a Cháit. Fód móna ó Mharcas Ó Conghaile is leaba chlúimh ó Mhichilín Crosach. Ára, cén chaoi a bhféadfadh sí leaba chlúimh a thabhairt léi ar bord loinge?

MICHILÍN: Agus 'measann tú nach fearr is nach téagarthaí í fúithi ná an fód móna a thug Marcas ar ball di?

MARCAS (*Go feargach*): Agus, a Mhichilín Crosach na gColm, cá bhfuair tusa clúmh? Ar ndóigh, ní raibh rud ar bith agatsa riamh ar fhás clúmh air. Ní fhaca duine ar bith beo ná marbh gé ná gandal agatsa riamh. Ach is cosúil gurbh é a ghoid a rinne tú.

MICHILÍN: Muise, tá a fhios ag an saol go raibh géabha is gandail agamsa chuile lá riamh, ach is cosúil nach raibh siad agatsa de réir an leasainm a tugadh ort. Ar ndóigh, níor glaodh riamh ort ach Marcaisín suarach na gCearc.

MARCAS: Hu, bíonn an chosúlacht ann. Is fada ó chlúmh a tógadh thú.

MICHILÍN: Bíonn an chosúlacht ann, a Mharcais. Is córa duit aire a thabhairt do do chruit!

MARCAS: Nár ba slán an scéalaí! Má tá cruit ormsa, is orm féin atá í a iompar. (*Féachann sé go fiochmhar ar Mhicheál*). Nach raibh dhá chruit ar d'athair nuair a tháinig sé as Meiriceá agus ní fhaca Dia ná duine i lár comhluadair gheanúil riamh é.

PEADAR: Sílim go bhfuil sibh fada go leor ag argóinteacht anois. Réitigh suas an teach, a Mhaighréad, go mbeidh céilí beag againn in ainm Dé.

MÁIRTÍN: Go díreach! Bíodh céilí againn in onóir don chailín gnaíúil atá ag imeacht go Meiriceá.

PEADAR: Sea, beidh amhrán againn i dtosach ó Mhicheál Mac Suibhne anseo. Is minic riamh a chuala sibh trácht ar Mhicheál. Anois, a Mhichíl, tabhair dúinn cúpla ceathrú den *Deoraí* go breá fuinniúil agus ansin beidh port againn ón bpíobaire.

CAOINEADH AN DEORAÍ[1]

Tá gleann beag ró-aoibhinn in Éirinn,
Agus baile beag talaimh sa ghleann;
Tá garraí beag bídeach chois coilleadh,
Agus cró beag ar foscadh faoi chrann.
Agus b'fhearr liom ná cumhacht na cruinne
A bheith ag seoladh thar sáile anonn –
Ach briseann mo chroí bocht le cumhaidh
Nach dtig liom níos mó a ghabháil ann.

Curfá:
Ach briseann mo chroí bocht le cumhaidh
Nach dtig liom níos mó a ghabháil ann.

Tá ardán in aice na coilleadh,
Agus tobar beag fíoruisce faoi,
Tá sruthán beag soilseach ag síneadh
Faoi bhruacha na sabharcán milbhuí;
Agus luífinn le lúcháir ag éisteacht
Le binnghlór na gcaochán sa ghleann,
Ach briseann mo chroí bocht le cumhaidh
Nach dtig liom níos mó a ghabháil ann.

Nach trua mé taobh seo na mara,
'Mo dheoraí gan beocht gan brí,
Ag smaoineamh ar aoibhneas na hÉireann
I measc coimhthígh gan carantas croí!

Ó, slán libh, a ghleannta mo thíre,
Agus slán libh, mo chúram is mo chró!
Nach buartha is nach brónach an scéal é
Nach féidir bhur bhfeiceáil níos mó.

Tar éis an damhsa a bheith tamall beag ar siúl cloistear torann ag an doras. Téann Cáit go bhfeice sí cé atá ann.

CÁIT: Dar fia, a dhaide, tá *Lady* ag an doras agus ba mhaith léi tú a fheiceáil.

PEADAR: Mise, an ea? *Lady*! Ára, cad é an tubaiste a thabharfadh *Lady* in mo thóirse? Glaoigh isteach uirthi go bhfeicimid céard tá ag teastáil uaithi nó cé hí féin.

Tagann an bhean uasal isteach.

AN BHEAN UASAL: Go mbeannaí Dia anseo.

PEADAR (*Ag féachaint go hiontach grinn uirthi*): Go mbeannaí Dia agus Muire duit, a bhean chóir. Suigh síos agus lig do scíth.

AN BHEAN UASAL: Go raibh míle maith agat, a Pheadair. Níl mé tuirseach. Inniu a tháinig mé abhaile as Meiriceá agus b'fhada liom go bhfaighinn aon amharc amháin ar na seanchomharsanaigh.

MAIGHRÉAD: Ní féidir go raibh tusa ins an gcomharsanacht seo riamh cheana.

AN BHEAN UASAL: Bhíos, muise, a Mhaighréad. Rugadh agus tógadh míle go leith as seo mé is ní féidir nach n-aithníonn ceachtar agaibh mé?

Siúd iad na comharsanaigh go léir ina haice go bhfaighe siad amharc níos fearr uirthi ach ní aithníonn ceachtar acu í.

EIBHLÍN NÍ ROIGHIN (*Tar éis féachaint uirthi arís*): Dar fia, cuimhním anois uirthi. Chomh cinnte is atá mé beo is tú Siobhán Ní Ruanáin a bhí ag dul ar scoil liomsa deich mbliana fichead ó shin.

AN BHEAN UASAL: Go deimhin ní rabhas, a Eibhlín, mar bhí tú 'do chailín óg is do ghruaig craptha nuair a bhí mise 'mo pháiste agus ní féidir go bhfuil mé ag féachaint chomh sean sin.

PEADAR: M'anam, muise, go bhfuil tú ag féachaint sean go leor, bail ó Dhia ort, pé bith rud a d'éirigh duit.

AN BHEAN UASAL: Ach tá sé chomh maith dom a inseacht daoibh cé mé féin. Is mise Máire Ní Eidhin a chuaigh go Meiriceá as Cnoc an tSeanbhaile deich mbliana ó shin.

Buaileann na comharsanaigh a lámha le chéile is, ar ndóigh, cuireann siad fáilte agus fiche roimpi.

MARCAS: Agus is tusa Máire Ní Eidhin! Céad slán don oíche a d'imigh tú – dhamhsaigh mé mo sháith i dteach d'athar.

PEADAR: Agus ní bréag ar bith nach tú Máire Ní Eidhin. M'anam gur tú a tháinig go tráthúil; níl sé leathuair an chloig ó bhíomar ag caint ort. Dúradh nach raibh aon bhean eile i Meiriceá chomh breá ná chomh saibhir leat; go raibh an oiread airgid agat agus a cheannódh dúthaigh Mhaigh Cuilinn ar fad; go raibh cóistí agus capaill is searbhóntaí ar mhullach a chéile agat; agus nach í an chulaith chéanna a d'fheicfí ort ar maidin a bheadh ort tráthnóna. An fíor é sin?

MÁIRE NÍ EIDHIN: Á, faraor, an lá ab fhearr a bhí mise i Meiriceá b'fhurasta mo chuid airgidse a chomhaireamh. Ach dá mbeadh an tsláinte agam, a Pheadair, ní dhéanfainn casaoid ar bith.

PEADAR: Muise, a Mhuire, is trua. Chonaic mise thú lá agus ba bhreá, gleoite, dathúil an cailín thú. Anois, faraor! Agus téann sé tríom é a rá, tá dath an bháis agus cuma an anó ort.

MÁIRE NÍ EIDHIN: Á, a Pheadair, is beag an t-ionadh dath an bháis a bheith ormsa. Ní chuile dhuine a dtéann an t-aer nó teas na gréine i Meiriceá go maith dó. Tá na céadta is na mílte a d'fhág an tír seo go láidir croíúil as a sláinte i Meiriceá, cuid acu ins na hospidéil, go leor eile i dtithe na mbocht, agus an chuid eile ar seachrán.

PEADAR: Má b'fhíor, a Mháire, nach raibh daoine bochta ar bith i Meiriceá.

MÁIRE NÍ EIDHIN: Hu, ná bí ag caint ar bhochtanas go dté tú go Meiriceá. Deir an cuntas is deireanaí atá poiblithe i dtaobh bochtanais ann go bhfuil níos mó daoine bochta as Éirinn ins na tithe déirce i Meiriceá ná mar atá as chuile thír eile sa domhan dá gcuirfí le chéile ar fad iad.

PEADAR: Dheamhan amhras agam ort, a Mháire.

MÁIRE NÍ EIDHIN: Níl i ndán do go leor Éireannach bocht i Meiriceá ach an sclábhaíocht agus an t-anó agus ní bhíonn obair sheasta acu. Nuair atá siad ina gcónaí, níl acu ach an teach déirce le dul ann.

PEADAR: Shílfeá, de réir cosúlachta, bail ó Dhia ort, nach obair éadrom a bhí ort féin.

MÁIRE NÍ EIDHIN: Is í an obair a bhí ormsa, a Pheadair, ag sciúradh an urláir agus ag glanadh an troscáin.

PEADAR: Ní hionann é sin, a Mháire, agus ag imeacht ar rothaí an tsaoil ar fud na mbailte móra mar a chualamar anseo.

MÁIRE NÍ EIDHIN: Mo léan géar! Is beag an baol go bhfágfainn an tír seo choíche murach litir mhallaithe a fuair mé is á rá dá dtéinn ann nach bhfeicfinn féin ná aon duine a bhain liom lá bocht go brách.

PEADAR: Há, há, bhí amhras agam gur ceann de na litreacha mallaithe seo ba chiontach leat a dhul ann. Ní bheidh rath ná rathúnas ar Éirinn go brách go ndéantar dlí a chuirfeas cosc leis na litreacha bréagacha seo. Is iomaí duine a fuair leithead a dhroma ar leaba phríosúin nach ndéanadh an ceathrú cuid as an mbealach agus atá na daoine a dhéanamh atá ag scríobh na litreacha seo.

MARCAS: Is cosúil nach n-airíonn tú thú féin go rómhaith in do shláinte, a Mháire.

MÁIRE NÍ EIDHIN: Faraor géar! Bhí mé ar fheabhas gur bhuail an tinneas cliabhraigh mé.

PEADAR: Ní fhéadfadh rud níos measa tú a bhualadh.

MÁIRE NÍ EIDHIN: Tá mé anois róchloíte agus rófhada tinn le biseach a fháil, agus níl súil ar bith agam le suaimhneas ná sólás an tsaoil seo. Ach tá súil agam, le cúnamh Dé, le m'anam a shábháil agus le mo chorp a bheith faoin bhfód in mo thír ghlas féin.

CÁIT: Ar ndóigh, chonaic tú do chol ceathar – Peig Mháirtín Sheáin. An fíor go bhfuil sí ina banoide agus í ag saothrú cúig *dollar* go leith sa ló ag múineadh clann boic mhóir?

MÁIRE NÍ EIDHIN: Ó, ná creid focal de sin. Níl sí ach ag sciúradh an urláir mar a bhí mé féin is ag glanadh na mbrat a bhíos air.

CÁIT: Muise, an gcreidfeá anois gurbh í Nóra a chuir an cháil sin amach oraibh ag iarraidh mise a mhealladh go Meiriceá ó mo mhama bhocht agus gan aici ach mé féin!

MÁIRE NÍ EIDHIN: Má ghlacann tú mo chomhairle, a Cháit, ní rachaidh tú go Meiriceá má tá slí ar bith mhaireachtála sa mbaile agat. Sin í mo bharúilse anois duit i dtaobh an mhéid atá le dul tríd agat i Meiriceá, is ná habair arís nár thug mé comhairle do leasa duit.

PEADAR: Ceist eile, a Mháire, agus ní bheimid 'do bhodhrú níos mó. An fíor go bhfuil Máirtín Beag Ó Ceallaigh a d'imigh as Baile na mBroc cúpla bliain ó shin ag saothrú deich fichead sa ló ina cheannfort nó ina stiúrthóir ar bhóthar iarainn is na mílte fear faoina chúram?

MÁIRE NÍ EIDHIN: Muise, go bhféacha Dia orainn! Tuilleadh de na bréaga. An bhfuil tusa 'do rí ar Éirinn?

PEADAR: M'anam, muise, nach bhfuilim, faraor – ná i ngar dó.

MÁIRE NÍ EIDHIN: Máirtín Beag Ó Ceallaigh ina stiúrthóir ar bhóthar iarainn! Tá Máirtín ina stiúrthóir ar a phiocóid nuair atá obair le fáil aige agus is maith uaidh úsáid a dhéanamh di.

PEADAR: Há, há, is deacair an seanrá a shárú: is glas iad na cnoic i bhfad uainn ach ní féarmhar. Níl a fhios agam beirthe ná beo cén fáth an mearbhall intinne seo atá ar mhuintir na hÉireann. Síleann siad má théann siad anonn go Meiriceá go bhfaighidh siad airgead faoina gcosa ach ní hamhlaidh atá – caithfidh siad é a shaothrú go crua, agus is iondúil, imíonn sé go holc. Tuige nach mbreathnaíonn siad thart timpeall orthu féin is féachaint ar na ceannaithe siopa is fearr agus is creidiúnaí sa tír seo, go dtáinig siad isteach ón tuath ina mbuachaillí beaga lena dtéarma a chaitheamh agus gur éiríodar saibhir gan bacadh le dul go Meiriceá ar chor ar bith.

Téann Maighréad agus Cáit ag cogarnach ar feadh tamaill bhig.

CÁIT: A athair dhílis, más mar sin a bheadh an scéal liomsa i Meiriceá, agus más fíor an méid a dúirt Máire Ní Eidhin i dtaobh na tíre sin – go gcaithfinn a bheith ag sciúradh, ag glanadh is ag sclábhaíocht, agus b'fhéidir gan dada dá bharr agam ach easpa sláinte agus fuarú creidimh, nach ormsa a bheadh an díth céille mo thír agus mo chairde a thréigeadh, b'fhéidir go broinne an bhrátha. Mar feicim gan amhras na daoine a thagann ar ais ón tír úd nach gcuireann siad suim ar bith in Aifreann, troscadh ná tréanas. Bíonn siad beagnach ina n-eiricigh! Buíochas le Dia, níl easpa ar bith ormsa faoi láthair. Ar an ábhar sin, sílim go nglacfaidh mé do chomhairle is go bhfanfaidh mé sa mbaile.

PEADAR: Mise i mbannaí, a Cháit, go bhfuil aiféala do sháith anois ort. Níl agat le déanamh ar an bpointe ach do phaisinéireacht a dhíol le pé bith cé a cheannós uait í.

CÁIT: Rachad suas go dtí an cabhróir agus iarrfad air í a dhíol dom.

MARCAS: Níl call agat an oiread sin trioblóide a fháil uaidh. Ceannóidh mise uait í, a Cháit, má fhaighim thú féin in éineacht léi.

CÁIT: Muise, go deimhin, a Mharcais, ní bhfaighidh tú mise ar an gcuntas sin ná ar chuntas ar bith eile, mar thug mise searc is grá mo chroí d'fhear óg cheana, is fear ar bith eile ach é ní phósfainn dá bhfaighinn a mheáchan féin d'ór leis.

MARCAS: Agus, a Cháit, a stór, cé hé an fear ádhúil sin, an bhfuil aon dochar é a fhiafraí?

CÁIT: Níl, muise. Sin é thall é – Máirtín Ó Roighin is ainm dó.

MARCAS (*Tar éis féachaint go grinn ar Mháirtín*): Muise, go bhfóire Dia ort, a Cháit, má chuireann tú (thú) féin amú ar fheithide shuarach mar é siúd! Féach mise a bhfuil mo ghabháltas breá talún agam agus gach ní eile dá réir, nach mbeadh call agat do lámha a shalú ó mhaidin go hoíche ach 'do shuí síos ar do chathaoir ag tabhairt airgead gaimbín amach don tír. Má phósann tú Máirtín beidh tú i mbochtanas go brách mar nach bhfuil luach a shuipéir aige.

MÁIRTÍN (*Ag éirí suas go feargach*): Mura bhfuil airgead ná ór agam, buíochas le Dia go bhfuil mo lámha agus mo shláinte agam lena saothrú! Ní bheinn mar thusa 'mo sheanchuaille sa gcoirnéal mar a bheadh cearc ar gor. A ghiolla na cruite agus a Shíle na gcearc, bheifeá ag comhaireamh na n-uibheacha uirthi.

MARCAS (*Ag croitheadh a chinn*): Bheadh siad agam le comhaireamh.

EIBHLÍN NÍ ROIGHIN: Seo, a Mháirtín. (*Ag síneadh sparán airgid chuige*): Ní raibh mise i Meiriceá ná i dtír ar bith eile ó rugadh mé ach bhí mé tíosach ar feadh mo shaoil agus chuir mé beagán airgid le chéile, agus ní ligfidh mé do sheanleibide, do sheanleiciméara mar é seo an ceann is fearr a fháil ortsa.

MÁIRTÍN: Muise, mo chuach óg ansin thú. Faraor nach bhfuil go leor de do leithéidese sa tír seo.

EIBHLÍN: Seo, tóg an sparán seo, a Mháirtín. Tá leathchéad punt ann agus ansin beidh cearca agus uibheacha agat chomh maith le Marcaisín suarach na gcearc.

MÁIRTÍN: Ó, mo sheacht ngrá ansin thú!

MARCAS: Dá bpósfadh sí mise ní bheadh sí i dtaobh le leathchéad punt!

EIBHLÍN: Ná bac leis an leathchéad punt, a Mharcaisín na gcearc, mar a ghlaoitear ort, an áit a bhfuil sé sin tá tuilleadh ann.

MARCAS: B'fhéidir dá n-íosfá leath do sháith an fhaid a bhí tú ag cruinniú an mhéid sin gur lú ná sin a bheadh agat.

CÁIT: Cogar mé seo leat, a Mharcais.

MARCAS: Sea, a Cháit, a stór.

CÁIT: Dá mbeifeá ag caint anois go gcaithfeá do theanga bheag, ba é an cás céanna duit é mar b'fhearr liomsa Máirtín gan bróg ar a chois ná tusa dá mbeadh airgead Déamair agat.

MARCAS: Go raibh maith agat, a Cháit. (*Ar leataobh*). Ach feicfidh tú féin nach mbeidh cead do chinn mar sin agat, a chailín. (*Féachann sé ar Pheadar*). Deirimse leat go mbeidh rud le rá ag duine éigin eile leis an gcúis seo.

Téann sé anonn go dtí Peadar ag cogarnach ina chluais.

MÁIRTÍN (*Le hathair na mná óige*): Cogar, a Pheadair, níl aon mhaith é a cheilt níos faide.

PEADAR: Céard é sin, a Mháirtín?

MÁIRTÍN: Tá a fhios ag an saol go bhfuil grá agamsa agus Cáit ar a chéile.

PEADAR: Má tá a fhios ag an saol é, a Mháirtín, nach mór an t-ionadh nach raibh a fhios agamsa air?

MÁIRTÍN: An dtabharfaidh tú d'iníon domsa, a Pheadair? Dheamhan pingin spré a iarrfas mé léi. Ní theastaíonn uaim ach í féin.

PEADAR: Dar fia, is crua an cheist í sin, a Mháirtín. Caithfidh mé comhairle na mná a ghlacadh i dtosach nó b'fhéidir go mbeadh aiféala orm ar ball. Ach déanfaidh mé mo dhícheall duitse ar chuma ar bith.

Téann sé féin agus Maighréad ag cogarnach ar feadh tamaill bhig. Téann Máirtín agus Cáit ag cogarnach freisin. Tabharann Máirtín an sparán airgid di i ngan fhios dóibh. Tá Marcas ag suí síos ag féachaint orthu agus é ag meilt a chuid fiacal.

PEADAR (*Ar leataobh le Maighréad):* Cé acu is fearr leat?

MAIGHRÉAD: Is fearr liom Máirtín. Tá sé ina bhuachaill gnaíúil agus tá leathchéad punt aige.

PEADAR: Is gearr a mhairfeadh leathchéad punt, nó céad punt ach an oiread.

MAIGHRÉAD: Is gearr a mhairfeadh míle punt dá gcuirfí drochrath air.

PEADAR: Ní chuirfidh Marcas drochrath ar an méid atá aige féin agus tá lán de chomhra mhór aige.

MAIGHRÉAD: Scread chasta air, an cruiteachán.

PEADAR: Is cosúil gurb é an freagra céanna a gheobhas mé uaithi féin.

CÁIT: Thug mise freagra a dhóthain do Mharcas cheana. Ní bheidh agamsa go brách ach Máirtín. Tá sé ina bhuachaill luath, láidir agus tá cion agus meas ar an áit a siúlann sé, ní hamháin air féin.

PEADAR: Cén mhaith é sin nuair nach bhfuil sé in ann bean a chothú?

CÁIT: Tá leathchéad punt aige is, b'fhéidir, le cúnamh Dé, go mbeadh an oiread den ádh ar an méid sin agus a bheadh ar an méid atá ag Marcas. Iarraim cead anois ort Máirtín a phósadh agus mura dtabhara tú cead dom, imeoidh mé go Meiriceá.

PEADAR: Déanfaidh sin. Ná bíodh níos mó ina thimpeall. (*Tar éis smaoineamh, le Máirtín*). Feicim anois go bhfuil grá agaibh ar a chéile agus bhéarfaidh mé duit í mar mhnaoi ach, mar sin féin, ní ligfidh mé amach folamh í. Bhéarfaidh mé fiche punt spré duit léi, cuingir ocsan is bodóg nuair a bhéarfas sí faoi Fhéile Pádraig le cúnamh Dé, agus ó tharla nár gheall Dia mórán talún duit, bhéarfaidh mé deich n-acra daoibh atá ansin thiar ag an gCnoc Bán a cheannaigh mé faoin mbille nua seo. Ansin, mura dtaga Seán abhaile as Mexico, beidh mo theach agus mo thalamh agat féin agus ag Cáit agus ag do shliocht 'do dhiaidh. Bheirim mo bheannacht anois le Dia a chur rath agus rathúnas, ádh agus iontar oraibh féin agus ar bhur maoin shaolta chomh fada agus a mhairfeas sibh.

MÁIRTÍN: Ó míle glóir le Dia! Ní raibh mé ag súil le leath an mhéid sin uait, a Pheadair.

PEADAR: B'aisteach an rud bean a thabhairt duit gan rud éigin léi.

MARCAS (*Ag éirí suas is deargbhuile air*): Cén diabhal a bhí orm teacht anseo ar chor ar bith! (*Leis féin*). Faraor géar, deacrach nach 'mo chodladh ar mo leaba a chuaigh mé! (*Le Cáit*). Bíodh sé agat anois, a Cháit, agus ní mór liomsa duit é, ach deirimse leat go n-íocfaidh tú ann lá is faide anonn ná inniu nuair a chuirfeas sé an cliabh aniar ar do chruit ag teacht an earraigh.

CÁIT: Má chuireann féin, a Mharcais, beidh mé in ann é a iompar.

MARCAS (*Le Máirtín tar éis féachaint go fíochmhar thart timpeall air*): Ára, a Mháirtín shuaraigh, b'fhurasta a aithne go raibh rud éigin eadraibh. B'fhurasta a aithne gur ar mhaithe leat féin a bhí tú is chomh cúramach is a bhí sibh faoi bhronntanais na gcomharsan ar ball! Tá aiféala orm anois m'fhód móna féin a thabhairt daoibh. Nach deas an teachtaireacht a thug mo chosa mé anseo anocht! (*Ag gáirí go fonóideach*). Agus nach deas an teachtaire a bhí mé a chur anonn go San Louis le cláirín! Cén dochar ach go dtí mo dheartháir geanúil!

Buaileann sé amach is glaonn Peadar air.

PEADAR: Ná bac leo, a Mharcais. Fan anseo más olc orthu é.

MARCAS (*Ag béicíl*): Lig chun bealaigh mé, a Pheadair, más é do thoil é. Ní fhanfainn anois ar chéad punt. Go deimhin, níl faice le rá agam leatsa agus tá súil agam go ngabhfaidh tú mo leithscéal faoin méid seo achrainn a tharraingt in do theach ach tá sé ag briseadh mo chroí tú a fheiceáil greamaithe le lucht na mbroghchán .i. muintir salach na mbroghchán nach raibh riamh in ann seasamh ag aonach ná ag margadh, ar chnoc ná ar ghleann, in éineacht le daoine geanúla.

Imíonn Marcas faoi dheireadh.

MÁIRTÍN: Buail bóthar anois, a ghiolla na cruite. Buail bóthar anois agus bain deatach as! (*Féachann sé ar Cháit*). Ó, míle glóir agus altú le Dia. Nach orm a bhí an t-ádh an chéad lá a casadh le chéile sinn.

CÁIT: Nach ormsa a bhí an t-ádh nach ndeachaigh go Meiriceá!

PEADAR: Beidh an t-ádh ar dhuine ar bith a ghlacfadh deachomhairle an aois (?)!

CÁIT: Leathchéad punt! Shíl mé nach raibh an méid sin sa mbaile ar fad.

PEADAR: Muise, muise. Shíl tú nach bhféadfaí airgead a dhéanamh in áit ar bith ach i Meiriceá. Dá gcuirfimis ár gcloigne le chéile agus úsáid a dhéanamh den intleacht bhreá a thug Dia dúinn, d'fhéadfaí airgead a dhéanamh in Éirinn chomh maith le háit ar bith eile sa domhan. Tá sé ins an uisce atá ag rith síos go díomhaoineach go dtí an fharraige, dá gcuirfí déantúis ar bun agus úsáid a dhéanamh de na muilte atá ina gcónaí ar gach taobh di. An fód móna a chonaic tú ansin ar ball, tá airgead ann dá ndéantaí é a chruadhú is úsáid a dhéanamh de i leaba an ghuail dhuibh, shalaigh sin atá ag teacht anall as Sasana ar bord loinge gach lá. Dá mbeadh deireadh leis an achrann seo atá idir na tiarnaí talún agus na tionóntaí agus feilm dheas, théagarthach a bheith ag chuile fhear tuaithe atá gan talamh ar bith faoi láthair – a chothódh é féin agus a mhuirín go breá compordach – tá súil agam nach mbeadh a leath oiread tóra ag na daoine ar dhul thar sáile agus a bhí ins an am atá caite. Go dtí sin, tá sé riachtanach ag gach fíor-Éireannach a lándícheall a dhéanamh chun na daoine a choinneáil sa mbaile, a bhfuil slí mhaireachtála sa mbaile acu, agus deireadh a chur go deo leis an leasainm suarach sin 'An Deoraí as Éirinn.'

Brat Anuas

Críoch

NÓTA

1 *'I have taken the liberty of embodying Prof. P.J. Craig's beautiful song in the play. It expresses the feelings of an Irish exile overcome by a spirit of loneliness in some far-off land, separated perhaps forever from home, family, and friends. Indeed it would be difficult to find a song more suitable for what has come to be known as the American Wake.* '– L. Ó T. (Tá an dán faoin teideal 'An Deoraidh' i gcló in *An Ceoltóir* (Báile Átha Cliath, 1904), 4–5.

Tá an dráma seo i gcló freisin in Éadaoin Ní Mhuircheartaigha agus Nollaig Mac Congáil (eagarthóirí), *Drámaí Thús na hAthbheochana* (Arlen House, 2008) 307–34.

The Exile

BY

Lorcan O'Toole

A Chairde,

The Exile is simply the well-known play *An Deoraí* in another dress.

It claims to be a faithful portrayal of the craze for emigration which hitherto has had such a terrible hold on the minds of the youth of Ireland, their idea being that they need only leave the green shores of Erin to realize a rapid fortune.

At the earnest request of numerous friends, and others who saw the need for an Anglo-Irish play on the subject of emigration, I have brought out *An Deoraí* in a form which makes it intelligible to those whose limited knowledge of the Irish language precluded them from reading the play in its original form.

Trusting that *The Exile* will meet with a favourable reception from the general public, and that the moral intended to be conveyed thereby, and so forcibly demonstrated by the story of the returned Yankee, will be seriously considered by the youth of this country.

Is mise,

Le meas mór,

LORCÁN Ó TUATHAIL

Muineachán, Meitheamh 1, 1907.

THE EXILE

Father	Peadar O'Donnell
Mother	Maighréad O'Donnell
Daughter	Cáit O'Donnell
Returned Yankee	Mary Hynes
Rejected Suitor	Marcus Fox (miser and gombeenman)
Successful Suitor	Máirtín O'Ryan
Aunt to Successful Suitor	Eibhlín O'Ryan

Village Schoolmaster, Neighbours, etc.

SCENE I

A farmer's kitchen. Cáit packing trunk for America, with the mother handing the things to her.

MOTHER: Take these, too, Cáit (*handing a pair of stockings*) that I spun and knitted from the wool of the black lamb you reared yourself when its mother died, and never mind those bought ones, that if your father saw he'd burn them in the fire.

CÁIT: And when I land in America and Nóra sees these (*holding homespun ones in her hand*) she'll do the same with them. So who am I to please?

MOTHER: Well, I'll say no more. You can please yourself.

CÁIT: Well, I'll put them in anyway, and sure they'll give Nóra a good laugh and make her think of old times at home.

Cáit retires from the kitchen. Mother lifts up the stockings and looks at them.

MOTHER (*Sorrowfully*): Oh, I spun them and knitted them. Aye, and I spun the light of my life and the joy of my heart along with them. Oh, *a leanbh bhán mo chroí*, will I ever see your face again on this side of the grave?

Lifts her apron to her eyes and leaves the kitchen sobbing as Cáit returns. Enter Father from the fair.

FATHER: Where's your mother, Cáit? I was delayed longer at the fair than I thought. Have you everything fed? (*In surprise*). Cáit, *a stór*, what are you packing this trunk for? Surely you are not starting for America so soon?

CÁIT: Indeed, father, I'm sorry I must, for I got the sailing ticket yesterday.

FATHER: Is it over the head of those few words we had the other day about you refusing to take Marcas na Cruite? But, Cáit, *a stór*, don't get it into your head that your father will ever force you to marry anyone against your will.

CÁIT: Indeed and it is not that, father, for I never thought of them since, or of Marcas either. It's little bother he was to me. But I must go on this ship anyhow, and what would I do staying here? Sure if I stayed my lifetime here, what would I have in the end only hardship and misery all the dear days of my life.

FATHER: Ah, now, Cáit, *a stór*, have some sense. Weren't you doing very well at home making 15s. a week at the lace class and never having a bit of need to do a hand's turn, only at it from morning to night.

CÁIT: Aye, but, father, what's 15s. a week? Sure it's nothing when you look at it. Wouldn't I earn that in one day in America?

FATHER (*Laughing scornfully*): Musha, would you indeed?

CÁIT: Well, sure I'd earn three times as much in the week anyhow.

FATHER: Arrah, whist, *a chuisle*; even if you would, too, when you pay your board and lodgings, what would you have, for they know well how to charge over there. It's not in ould Ireland you'll be, for there is nothing for nothing in it, by all accounts.

CÁIT: Well, there's no use in us talking more now, for I must go anyhow. Sure didn't you see the letter Nóra sent home a fortnight ago?

FATHER: Aye, and what about that?

CÁIT: Didn't she say she wouldn't be content if I wouldn't go?

FATHER: How does that come?

CÁIT: She's so lonesome for someone to talk to.

FATHER: Bedad, that's very quare. Sure it isn't a month since she wrote home that she was as content as the flowers of May.

CÁIT: Aye, but didn't she change to another place since?

FATHER: Well, Cáit, if she did, the place she was in mustn't have been what she was saying it was or she wouldn't be leaving it so soon.

CÁIT: Oh, I never thought. Wait till I read the letter for you that I got from Nóra today. Maybe it would change your mind a bit about America.

Pulls out letter and proceeds to read it as mother enters.

FATHER: Bedad, I was thinking you got something that was hurrying you off, but I have my doubts but it is another of the lying letters that's doing so much harm in the country, coaxing away the youngsters, even if it is from my own daughter itself.

CÁIT (*Reading*): 3,478 Bedlam Avenue, Canning Town, USA.

A Cháit, Don't be listening to them that tell you to stay at home.

FATHER: What, not even to your own father?

CÁIT: *What are you, but poor slaves in Ireland! God help you, trudging from morning to night. You'll be a gran' high-up lady here. Look at me. I wouldn't go back to Ireland now if I got all the money in Pinchin's Bank. I have a grand carpet under my feet that you'd bog in from I rise in the morning till I go to bed at night.*

FATHER: Aye, and not an inch of it her own.

CÁIT: *There's nothing under you but the cold, clay floor.*

FATHER: Well, that's our own anyway.

CÁIT: *As for the money, it is as plentiful as the blackberries in harvest. I heard a man that knows a good bit saying the other day that there is twice as much money here as they can make use of, and that America yet will be that they'll think no more of money than you would of the stones on the road in Ireland - .*

FATHER: Bedad, we should go over for an odd shipful; it would be better than the canned stuff they send over. But, go on.

CÁIT (*Reading*): *It's no lie but the neighbours are doing well here. Of course you mind Mary Hynes that went out of Lisaraw not long ago.*

FATHER: A nice wee girl she was.

CÁIT: *If you saw her now you'd think she was the Lord Lieutenant's wife, with all the grandeur there is on her. She hasn't to wet her shoes crossing the street, and she has her carriage and horses to bring her from one end of the city to the other. She has a houseful of servants and coachmen to wait on her, and she can put on a fresh dress every hour in the day.*

FATHER: Stop, Cáit. If that's true she must have married a millionaire. One of them Rockfellers.

CÁIT: *She has a big gold chain round her neck that would tether McCaffrey's goat, and the shoes on her feet cost five dollars and a half. They have heels on them the length of your hand, and soles just like threepenny bits. Boys do well here, too. There's wee Máirtín Lannigan. I'm sure you often heard of him. He has eight dollars a day – a gaffer on a railway – with as many men under him as would be at first Mass on Christmas morning. When he was at home he was drawing turf with an ass and creels and without a shoe to his foot. Now, he has a gold watch in his pocket, at one hundred and fifty dollars, with a chain to it as thick as a cross rope on a hay pike. But, to conclude, if you wish to remain a slave, stop in Ireland; but if you want to be making money like jackstones, come right out here at once. Yours etc., Nóra.*

FATHER: Bedad, I often heard of 'well and doing well – like an American letter' – but that beats all. Cáit, *a ghrá*, is there any more lies in it?

CÁIT: Well, father, you surprise me. Can't you speak with some sense? I'm sure Nóra isn't telling a word of lie.

MOTHER: Well, in troth, it sounds like the truth; and I'm sure, Peadar, it's not on your own child you'd be saddling a lie.

FATHER: Sounds like the truth! Aye, indeed, the truth! (*To himself*). Oh, the lie is sometimes told when truth does not suit.

MOTHER (*Reproachfully*): Oh, you wouldn't believe the bishop if he were to speak again you.

FATHER: *Éist do bhéal, a deirim leat* or I'll leave the house this minute. Don't you think the people are great fools? (*Thinking*). By the holy farmer, but if Máirtín's story is true, it beats all I ever heard, but I won't grudge it to him, poor fellow.

MOTHER: No, nor me neither; but, in truth, if he has the half of it he should think of his poor mother that would be in the poorhouse long ago, only for the goodness of the neighbours.

CÁIT: Maybe he's drinking it, the ruffian.

FATHER: Whist, don't be so hard on any poor fellow, with all your talking; maybe he hasn't as much as would pay his passage home, and sure if he has, all the better for himself, but time will tell.

CÁIT: Well, I'm going over now to leave farewell with old Peggy. I'm sure only for the pains in her bones she'd be the first here tonight. So *beannacht libh go fóill*.

Goes out.

MOTHER: *Go soirbhí Dia duit, a leanbh*.

MOTHER (*Again, looking after Cáit*): Musha, Peadar, but she'll be a grand lady, out and out, over in America.

FATHER: Oh, don't be bothering me. (*Scornfully to himself*). A grand lady, indeed! A fig for your grand ladies!

MOTHER: Now, what's vexing you, or what are you so cross and angry for?

FATHER (*Crossly*): Ye're as bad as another! Wouldn't it be better for herself and the whole of us for her to stay at home?

MOTHER: I won't say another word more about it; let her do what she likes.

FATHER (*Passionately and flinging the chair from him*): Do what she likes, indeed! It's no wonder she's spoiled, and it's often you said that to her.

MOTHER: It's not me spoiled her if she's spoiled. Was it me spoiled Seán too, when he stole away in the middle of the night and took the £20 with him out of the chest, and ran away to California where, the Lord save us, I'm towl' the earth opens and swallows the people sometimes.

FATHER: Much good may it do him. He took nothing but what he earned hard and sore, and he was the boy was neither lame nor lazy to earn it.

MOTHER: That's not what you said when he went away.

FATHER: Well, if I said anything hard of him it was because my temper got the better of me at the time, and it wasn't much wonder that I was angry and him the only son I had in the world. (*Thinks*). £20 indeed! And how far will it be off £20 more when this rendezvous is over tonight and Cáit left on the big ship. (*Shouting loudly*). If God hasn't said it, it will put me out of house and home.

MOTHER (*Soothingly*): With the help of God, it won't. Sure this is a night by itself. Now, for Heaven's sake, send her off decently and don't make a country's talk of us.

FATHER: Musha, indeed, a lot I care about the talk; aren't they talking as it is for letting her go at all? There's nothing nowadays but 'when had you a letter from America? When are you going? Hurry up and give us a spree'. That's the whole talk amongst the youngsters once they're able to earn a shilling.

MOTHER: Arrah, whist, Peadar. Don't be talking that way, but go and ask the neighbours.

FATHER: Do what you like; send for the whole country, and make a regular *margadh mór* of it.

Father goes out.

MOTHER: Oh, God keep me. God, this day and this night.

CURTAIN

SCENE II

Father sitting smoking. Mother 'cleaning up'.

CÁIT (*Enters dressed as if for America*): I sent for them all but Marcas na Cruite.

FATHER: And why did you leave Marcas behind?

CÁIT: Well, I was thinking he'd come himself without being asked. Who ever saw him missing anything here?

FATHER: No matter for all that he's the first man I'd ask.

MOTHER: Aren't you a lot unaisy about Marcas? Whoever saw anything in his own house? There's not that much good in him.

FATHER: Well, do you mind last year when I searched the whole country looking for potato diggers and couldn't get one, and he came, when even your own brother stayed at home and him near done digging at the time? Now, put that in your pipe and smoke it.

MOTHER: It wasn't to oblige you or me he come; he had something else in his eye.

FATHER: Well, if he had, too. Did you ever hear the old saying: *ar mhaithe leis féin a dhéanas an cat crónán* – 'it's for the good of himself the cat purrs'. But, after all, only for him where would you be? You wouldn't have a pratee out of the ground.

MOTHER: Much about all he was able to dig; you could carry them on your back from this to Monaghan.

FATHER: No matter, that ends it. I will go for him anyway.

Goes out.

MOTHER: Well, you are going now, Cáit, and it's the same thing to send you to America as to send you to the grave.

CÁIT: Mother, *mo chroí*, don't say that. Won't I be taking yous all out next year?

MOTHER: Send for us as soon as you can, for it's little of the world's comfort I'll have after you. But, till you can do that, Cáit, *a stór*, write every week, for, empty or full, there'll always be a welcome for your letter.

FATHER (*Entering*): There will and a *céad míle fáilte* for it, although it breaks my heart to see her laving me.

MOTHER: But what about Marcas? I thought you'd have him here by this.

FATHER: And so he is. I saw him coming over here. Aren't you there, Marcas?

MARCAS: Oh, indeed I am here, Peadar. God save all here, except the cat.

FATHER: How is every inch of you, Marcas?

MARCAS: There's no use in grumbling (*Looks round him*). Peadar, I thought the house would be full and I see no one here yet. Surely Cáit isn't gone away, for I'd like to have another chat with her, and, in troth, I come over in sich a hurry that I never thought of milking, and, bedad, I'll have a tough job getting it done when I go home. But, sure, it serves me right when I didn't get somebody long ago.

FATHER (*Shouting to Cáit*): Come here, Cáit.

CÁIT: Yes, father.

FATHER: Be friendly to Marcas now.

CÁIT: *Céad míle fáilte, a Mharcais.*

MARCAS: Thank ye, Cáit, *a thaisce*. You're laving tonight and that you may have good luck and God's blessing every day you rise, and sure you will, with the help of God, for it's you had everyone's good word since you left the cradle, and there wasn't a wee girl ever left the country I had the same regard for as I had for you.

CÁIT: *Go raibh maith agat, a Mharcais.* It's me that'll send you the nice pipe and big roll of tobacco every Christmas.

Enter Máirtín O'Ryan and his aunt. The aunt [is] taken into the parlour.

MÁIRTÍN (*To Peadar*): *Go mbeannaí Dia anseo.*

Shakes hands with Peadar.

FATHER: *Dia is Muire dhuit, a dhuine chóir.*

Peadar goes off the scene and Máirtín enters and sees Marcas looking at a piece of old newspaper.

MÁIRTÍN (*Aside*): Och, holy Moses, if here isn't Marcas na Cruite already. Can it be possible he has still a notion of Cáit? Well, well, an ould fool is always the worst. But Marcas did not come so early without expecting to make something of it. (*Taps Marcas on the shoulder and speaks*). *Cad é mar atá tú, a Mharcais*? (*Marcas grunts*). By my word, you came in a hurry. Why I saw you at your work not half an hour ago.

MARCAS: I suppose you'd rather not see me here. I'm a thorn in your side, my boyo.

MÁIRTÍN: Why, you poor, miserable, whining, old miser – what do I care where you are or where you aren't; but I am very sure you did what no one does coming to a place of this kind – come with your hands as long as [each] other.

MARCAS: What have you under that, Máirtín?

MÁIRTÍN (*Scornfully*): What have I under that? Oh, you are got very innocent of a sudden. Answer me this, Marcas. Have you a present for Cáit?

MARCAS: Have you one yourself, Máirtín?

MÁIRTÍN: That's not the way to answer my question – but I'm answered at any rate. Your heart wouldn't let you – you old, miserable miser (*Walks to the other side of the room indignantly*).

MARCAS (*To himself*): If I liked I could give her the weight of herself in yellow gold, but I'm not such a --- fool as all that. Still, it might coax her like to give her something, and I could have it all back again – and herself along with it. I think I will risk a little present. (*Aloud, very coaxingly*) – Máirtín! (*No reply. Rises and moves over to Máirtín*). Máirtín, I say, Máirtín!

MÁIRTÍN (*With disdain*): Well, what's troubling you now?

MARCAS (*Straightening himself up very proudly*): What would A MAN LIKE ME be supposed to give?

MÁIRTÍN (*Looks him all over a couple of times and breaks out laughing*): A man like you (*looks at him again*) – A man like you – och, anything at all – anything you like. I'll guarantee you won't hurt your pocket much anyhow.

Marcas goes out muttering to himself: 'Anything at all'. Cáit enters and goes over to Máirtín. Máirtín gives Cáit a handsome present and holds her hand and says:

MÁIRTÍN: *Mo bhrón, mo bhrón, a Cháit, a mhuirnín.* It's little I thought the present I'd be giving you would be for the other side of the broad Atlantic.

CÁIT: And it's little I thought it meself either. But Nóra says it's a fine place, and maybe you'd come out too.

MÁIRTÍN: Cáit, *a leanbh,* I don't wish to dishearten you, but I don't know what opinion to have about that letter of Nóra's. Didn't we hear many and many a time from Father – that there are thousands starving in America and Chicago, of all places in the world, where they say, God bless us, they are grinding up people and making sausages iv them.

Neighbours come in and interrupt conversation between Máirtín and Cáit. They all give presents. They sit round the kitchen and chat on local topics and pass jokes. All the girls come in from the parlour – where they have got refreshments – and as the dance is about to start in comes Marcas na Cruite with a sod of turf for a present. Máirtín sees him and makes up to him, saying:

MÁIRTÍN: Why, Marcas, are you back so soon? Sorra long you were. What is this you have got with you? (*Marcas looks at him angrily and in his haste drops the sod. Máirtín makes a dart for it, and holds it up for all to see, saying*): Oh, gracious goodness, will you all look! Was ever such a present seen for a girl? A wet, rushy, bog sod. (*All laugh*). But I suppose it broke his heart to part with that much atself. I'll wager a shilling he didn't dig it on his own land. Did you, Marcas?

MARCAS: Well, I didn't then. I'd give her more than that.

CÁIT: I'm as thankful to you as if you had brought me the whole bog-hole.

MARCAS (*Elated*): Do you hear that now, Máirtín? She's just as thankful as if you had kept your mouth shut.

Some sharp interchanges take place between Máirtín and Marcas which the master interrupts.

MÁIRTÍN: Whist, whist, here is the schoolmaster.

SCHOOLMASTER: *Bail ó Dhia is Muire oraibh.*

FATHER: *Céad míle fáilte.*

SCHOOLMASTER: Thank you, Peadar. Where's Cáit? I would like to have a few words with her before she goes.

Enters Cáit and welcomes the master.

SCHOOLMASTER: *A Cháit, a stór,* you're leaving us tomorrow. You're going to face the cold stranger in a distant country, and my earnest wish and prayer to you, Cáit, *a leanbh,* is that you may never forget the principles of religion and the traditions of the Gael; and though it grieves me to see you leaving the green shores of Erin, yet in the place you are going to you can do a good deal for your motherland. There is one thing you can do with advantage to yourself and to Ireland, and that is to learn the Irish language, the study of which you have already begun under my poor tuition.

CÁIT: I will do that, master; and I will try to induce others to do the same.

The master, going aside, opens a little parcel of books and talks to himself.

MASTER: I would like to give her something more valuable than a few old, second-hand books, but I can't afford it. I'm getting it as tight as nails, and no wonder – to keep up appearances and maintain a wife and family on the magnificent stipend of a 'quid' a week. Why, I can't afford to buy a decent overcoat, but have to content myself instead with an umbrella. Then, of course, the bountiful British Government expects me to be loyal and toast the King's health at a teachers' *céilí*.

(*Speaking aloud*): Here, Cáit, *a stór*, is a present of some books for you. I'm sorry I haven't a valuable present to give to you. However, I trust you will appreciate the gifts, not from their intrinsic value, but from the amount of instruction and amusement which I am sure you will derive from their perusal, for they are works of a very entertaining character – all relating to Ireland.

Cáit returns thanks to the master.

FATHER (*To the master*): Have you become acquainted with our very welcome and highly-respected guest, Marcas Fox, from Drumhilla?

MASTER: No, but I've heard of him. How are you, Mr. O'Shanaghy? (*Aside to Máirtín*). Isn't this the old miser that goes by the name of Marcas na Cruite?

MÁIRTÍN: The very man. His real name is Fox.

MASTER: The name suits him well by all accounts.

MÁIRTÍN: Too true for you. There isn't a fox that ever got a grip of a goose could bate him in cuteness.

FATHER: Well, master, how're the scholars doing?

MASTER: They're doing well, Peadar – those that come regular to school; but the job is to get them to go. It is highly deplorable, indeed, the large percentage of children that are kept at home doing nothing.

MÁIRTÍN: Nothing at all. There's gosoons left at home now that's doing nothing, barrin' tarin' wan another's clothes in the hedges.

NEIGHBOUR: Ye're talking now about eddication and gran' larnin', but there's Marcas, that never stood inside a school in his life and was never taught to add two and two together – yet I'd like to see the man that could do him out of a penny of gombeen money.

MÁIRTÍN: A fig for him and his ill-got money. Sure he can't sleep at night but thinkin' about it.

FATHER: How are they getting on with the Irish, master?

MASTER: They are getting on well.

FATHER: That's encouraging.

MASTER: It is. It's a good sign for the future of the language that the youngsters who are growing up now are being taught their native tongue.

Marcas, who is engaged in the arranging of some old papers, looks around when he hears the word Irish mentioned.

MARCAS: I hear ye always talkin' about Irish. Well, what's it all about? What Irish is it?

All the company laugh.

FATHER: This is the Irish language, Marcas – the language that was spoken long ago, when Ireland was famous for larnin' all over the world.

MARCAS: Arrah, Peadar, sure there is no money to be made out of that kind of nonsense.

MASTER: Surely there are higher aims in life than making money, and even you, miser and all as you are, will very shortly be glad you had learned it, when you are not able to understand what the people are saying around you.

MARCAS: And that's what ye're teaching the gossoons. Faith, then, ye'll have a tough job of it; but fire away and let me not interrupt you in your song.

Master sings.

MARCAS: And is that the Irish, Peadar? Is that the thing ye're learning them? It sounds nice anyway. But what was id about?

MASTER: It's about the exile's lament for leavin' his native home!

MARCAS: Yes, but I don't understand a word iv it. How long would a body be larnin' it? Pick it up in a night or so?

All laugh.

MASTER: I'm afraid not but you should come anyhow – maybe you'd pick up something.

MARCAS (*To Peadar*). Begob, I'll go down to hear them at it anyway, if I can get away from doin' things about the house.

Dances, recitations, songs etc. are gone through. The céilí being interrupted by a knock at the door.

CÁIT: Father, there's a lady at the door to see you.

FATHER (*Exclaims*): Is it me? What does a lady want with me? Bring her in anyway till we see her.

Enter lady.

LADY: Good night to all you folks.

FATHER (*Surprised*): Good night, my good woman. Sit down and rest yourself, ma'am.

LADY: Thank you very much, Peadar, but I guess I'm not very tired. I came home from America today and I longed to get a sight of my old neighbours once more.

MOTHER: It can't be possible that you were ever in this country before?

LADY: Well, I guess I was. I was bred and born not half a mile from here, and surely some of you must know me.

EIBHLÍN (*Looking sharply*): Throth, I think I know her. As sure as I'm standing here, you're Susan McTague that was at the wooden school at Carnmore thirty years ago with me.

LADY: I guess you're wrong. You were a *cailín óg* with your hair in a ball when I was a-rocking in the cradle, and it can't be that I look so old as all that.

FATHER: 'Pon my sowl, you look ould enough, but it's more like hardship than ould age whatever the dickens has come over ye.

LADY: Well, I guess I'd better inform you who I am. I'm Mary Hynes that went from Lisaraw ten years ago.

Neighbours clap and give her a céad míle fáilte.

MARCAS: And you're Mary Hynes. God be with the night I danced my fill in your father's house.

FATHER: Not a lie in it but you're Mary Hynes. Begob, you came in time. Speak of the ---- and he'll appear. It isn't half an hour since we were talking about you. It was said here you had the weight of yourself in yellow goold; that you had coaches and horses and servants to wait on you thripping one another, and that you were hardly ever seen twice in the same shuit. Is that true?

LADY: Indeed it isn't, Peadar. The best day ever I saw in America you could easy count my dollars; but if I had my health I'd never complain.

FATHER: Musha, musha, more's the pity. The day I saw you going, it's little I thought I'd ever see you as you are now. Before you went away you were a blooming, rosy-cheeked girl, and it's little I thought such a change could come over you.

LADY: Oh now, it's all very well going to America, but it is a different story when you are there a while. I guess and calculate it's not everyone can stand the climate over there, along with the pressure of stylish Yankee life, and I guess I may thank my stars that I was able to come over here to see all you folks again, and you'd bet your bottom dollar there were plenty of folk went out there as strong and as hardy as I was, and they'd be bloomin' well glad to come home if they could knock up enough dollars to take them.

FATHER: Divil a bit I'd doubt it.

LADY: You bet a poor greenhorn going over there must rough it a bit. I guess they think leaving home that they have nothing to do only run a saloon, or drive a trolly car, but they'll bloomin' well soon find that they've got left.

FATHER: By your accounts the work must be a holy terror.

LADY: Well, I guess I'll just tell you what I was doing, and, by jove, I think it will open your eyes a bit about life over there.

FATHER: Well, Mary, *a stór*, just let us hear it.

LADY: Well, the work I was at was scrubbing the floors and cleaning the furniture and doing general work in a kitchen two storeys underground.

FATHER: By my conscience, that's different from driving in a motor car as we were a-leading to believe a while ago.

LADY: *Mo bhrón go deimhin,* I'd have never left Ireland only for a letter I got from my aunt and she, too, was rolling in riches, and she told me when I'd get on the other side I'd never see a poor day again. But I guess it was quite different when I got out there. She very soon showed me I had got to look out for myself, but I couldn't blame her for that as she was getting it as tight as nails to make out for herself. The only thing I could blame her for was for not telling me the truth in time.

FATHER: Ha, ha! I always 'dubioused' that the American letters were all a bundle of lies, but now I am sure and certain for I have the proof of it.

CÁIT: Did you hear about your first cousin, Peggy Martin? Is it true she is a governess with a millionaire?

LADY: Well, by jove, I guess you folks make me smile. Now, don't believe any such bosh. Peggy is living with a family right enough out Jersey way, but you bet it's not TEACHING she is. She has got to WHEEL an old lady through the PARK, and attend to her, and I tell you that's not all sunshine.

CÁIT: Musha, would you believe it, it was our Nóra sent home that word about you when she was coaxing me out there, and wanting me to leave my poor mother desolate in the end of her days.

LADY: Well, Kate, if you take my advice you'll not go to America, if you find any way of near living at home for I haven't told you the half of it. I could tell you things that would make the hair stand on your head.

FATHER: Well, another question, Mary, and I'm done asking. Is it true that wee Máirtín Lannigan of Drumaclan is head gaffer on the Pacific Railway, with as many men under him as would be at a Gooseberry Fair in Monaghan?

LADY: Musha, God help your foolish wit. That's another Yankee bouncer. I might as well say you are Lord Mayor of Dublin.

FATHER: By me sowl, then, I'm not. I'm far off it.

LADY: Máirtín is gaffer over a pick and shovel, and if he got constant work, a fine wee fellow he'd be and a good worker.

FATHER: Ha, ha, I often heard it said that 'cows in Connaught have long horns' and 'hills are green far away'. I don't know from Adam what's putting the craze for America and other foreign countries on the Irish boys and girls. They think there's money for the liftin' but in troth I see they make a big mistake, for they have to earn it hard an' sore; 'tis often it goes badly. There's plenty to be made at home if they'd work for it half as hard.

CURTAIN

SCENE III

Mother and daughter (in kitchen).

CÁIT: If that is the way the story goes and if what Mary Hynes says is true, that I'd have to be a regular slave in America and reap no reward but bad health, and maybe not get to Mass on Sunday, wouldn't I be the foolish girl to forsake my country and friends, perhaps for ever. I often see many people coming out of it that care nothing for either God or man. Thanks be to God there is nothing wanting here at home, and for that reason I'll take your advice and live and die in holy Ireland.

FATHER: I never heard anything I am prouder to hear. You have only now to return your passage ticket.

MARCAS: You need not bother yourself about your ticket; I will buy it off you if you only let me get yourself into the bargain.

CÁIT: Well, indeed, Marcas, I'll have no bargain of the kind, for my heart and hand are pledged to another, and none but him will I have.

MARCAS: And, Cáit, *a stór*, who may that lucky one be, if it's any harm to ask?

CÁIT: It is not a bit of harm, Marcas, there he is. Máirtín O'Ryan is his name.

MARCAS (*Looking sharply at Máirtín*): Musha, God help you, Cáit, if you throw yourself away on a poor divil like that. Look at me that has the best place in the parish with not as much as a stone to throw at a dog, and the grass growing over the ditches; with me you'd be a lady, not having a hand's turn to do but sitting in your parlour lending out gombeen money from morn to night. If you take Máirtín, you'll live to rue the day, a man that hasn't the price of his supper.

MÁIRTÍN (*Rising indignantly*): If I have not gold or silver like you, thank God I have a head to plan and hands to work, and a heart that is not consumed in the love of filthy lucre. I would not be like an old henwife – disposed to count the eggs before they are laid. Clever would be the woman who could eat one unknown to you.

MARCAS (*Shaking his head*): Thank God that I have eggs to count and hens to lay them.

AUNT (*Rising and handing purse to Máirtín*): I was never in America but, with industry and frugality, I have saved this little hoard, and I won't allow this *cruiteachán* to get the better of you. (*To Máirtín*). Here are £50 for you, and you'll have something to start you in the world.

MÁIRTÍN: God spare you, aunt.

MARCAS: If she married me she would not be confined to £50.

AUNT: You need not despise £50. There is more where that came from.

MARCAS (*To himself*): I wonder where she got the £50. I nearly starved myself to death gathering my stocking. (*Looks at aunt*). Devil a much sign of starvation on her.

CÁIT: Whisper me this, Marcas.

MARCAS: Yes, Cáit, *a stór*.

CÁIT: If you were talking to Tibb's Eve, it is all the same, for I'd rather have Máirtín without a shoe to his foot than you if you had the wealth of Croesus, for I don't care about you.

MARCAS: I'm oblidged to you, Cáit; but, be my sowl, you haven't it all your own way yet. (*Aside, after looking at Peadar*). This match won't go on without the father's consent, and I don't think Peadar will give his daughter to a labouring boy like Máirtín O'Ryan. (*Goes over to Peadar and talks to him*).

MÁIRTÍN: Peadar, might I speak to you a minute? There's no use in beating about the bush any longer. Cáit and I have a great *grá* for one another.

FATHER: Begorra, that's the first I ever knew about it.

MÁIRTÍN: Well, Peadar, will you give her to me? I'm asking nothing with her. All I want is herself.

FATHER: Bedad, that's not an easy question to answer. I must consult with the ould woman about that or I might be sorry bye and bye. Home Rule isn't the thing you think, as you'll likely find out when you're a while married.

Father and mother converse in private. Máirtín and Cáit converse. Máirtín gives Cáit the purse. Marcas looks on with a grin, in suspense.

FATHER: So you prefer Máirtín.

MOTHER: I do. I didn't care about him at first as I thought it nonsense when he had only his day's work to support him, but now he has £50 and that's a very good start.

FATHER: Marcas has twenty times £50.

MOTHER: Much about his money, the ould miser. It'll melt yet.

CÁIT: Now, father, there's no use in any more talk about Marcas, for I'd beg before I'd marry him, the ould skinflint.

FATHER (*Aside*): Begorra, I'll pretend I didn't give in yet or maybe the old woman would change and go for Marcas, and, in troth, that's a match I don't want, for I wouldn't force Cáit again' her will for all the money in the Bank of England, and what's money and riches anyhow? (*Looks at Marcas*). And, begorra, I am a better-looking man than Marcas myself.

MARCAS *(Smiling scornfully)*: Ha, ha, ha, you'll cry that yet, some day.

CÁIT: See here, Marcas, I gave you your answer long ago. I'll never marry a decrepid, old miser that's older than my father. Why, it is saying your prayers you ought to be. (*To the father*). Father, will you give your consent to my marrying Máirtín O'Ryan that has the love of my heart this many a day, and is as much liked by everyone as Marcas is hated.

Máirtín whispers.

CÁIT: And if you don't, I'll just pack up and start for America.

FATHER (*To himself*): That's what I was waiting for. Isn't it a wonder they didn't think of it sooner? (*Father speaks to Cáit*). Very well, that ends it. I see you're fond of each other and it would be a sin to separate you. (*To Máirtín*). I'll give her to you and won't send her off empty-handed either. It'll never be said that Peadar married his daughter without a fortune. How much do you want?

MÁIRTÍN: Peadar, I'm no fortune hunter. I have only my health and my hands to keep Cáit, and with God's help they're able to do it, so I ask nothing but her own sweet self.

FATHER: Aisy, Máirtín, I'm a fairly well-to-do man so I'll give you the new farm, 10 acres, I got in Rawe from the Estate Commissioners, and three score pounds to put horses on it, the strawberry heifer that's coming in May, and ten good sheep and my blessing into the bargain.

MÁIRTÍN: It's too much, Peadar, far too much.

FATHER: I always said I'd give her a good fortune if she'd stay at home and marry some honest, respectable boy, and though I never thought of you till tonight, there's not a boy in the country I'd sooner trust my daughter's happiness to.

MARCAS (*In a rage to himself*): What the devil kept me here at all? I wish to God I had gone home to my bed. (*To Cáit*). I don't begrudge you your happiness – all you'll have of it. Be my sowl, he'll put the creel on your back yet instead of his own, and that he may never miss.

CÁIT: No danger of that, and sure I'm able to carry the half of the load any day.

MARCAS (*To Máirtín*): It's aisy knowing why you were so smaisy about Cáit getting presents. I am sorry I didn't burn the sod of turf.

Marcas goes out and Cáit hits him with the turf.

FATHER: What's your hurry, Marcas? Make your *céilí*, man.

MARCAS: I must go, Peadar. I am sorry for raising a row in your house. But it's breaking my heart to see your daughter married to one of the O'Ryans – that one belonging to him wouldn't be let into the same place with you or me.

MÁIRTÍN (*Walking over threateningly*): You'd better be moving, you libel on the name of humanity. If I thought it worth my while, I'd straighten your back across my knee. (*To Cáit*). Thank God he's gone. We'll have peace now.

CÁIT: And thank God that I didn't go to America.

FATHER: And from my heart I thank God, too, for nothing ever went to my heart so much.

A stranger comes to the door carrying a portmanteau. Peadar, who recognises him immediately as his own son, Seán, exclaims:

FATHER: Oh, Seán, Seán, Seán!

SEÁN: Father, father, father!

Father and son embrace each other.

SEÁN: Father, I have just escaped from the earthquake in San Francisco. I have lost everything I had in the world. I was so hard up that I had to work my passage home. I had to walk half the way. I promise you I'll never go there again anyhow. I'll tell you all when I have time.

FATHER: Thank God you brought your life out of it, whatever ye lost ... May this be the last of the American wakes, and, if there be another one, may it turn out as happily as this has done. For, be it ever so humble, there is no place like home.

THE END

DÓNALL DIAGANTA

Dráma Trí Ghníomh

a chum

Labhrás Ó Tuathail

An Fhoireann:

Séamas Ó Durcáin (atá ag troid in aghaidh Rialtas Shasana)

Siobhán (máthair Shéamais - Baintreach)

Caitlín (deirfiúr Shéamais – Cailín Óg)

Dónall Diaganta (atá ina chara (mar dhea) do Mhac Uí Dhurcáin)

Tadhg (seoinín suarach atá ag cur isteach ar bheith ina ghiúistís)

Uilliam Ó Dubháin (Maor Thigh na mBocht – Deartháir Thaidhg)

Úna (Cócaire Thigh na mBocht)

An Grugaire (Cúntóir an Mhaoir)

Diarmuid Crom (Cúntóir an Mhaoir)

Páidín Ó Maoláin (.i. Séamas Ó Durcáin)

Cormac Mac an Bhaird — Seachránaithe Bochta

Conall na gCaorach

Peadar Leisciúil agus a bhean Nuala

Éamann na gCos (Cláiríneach Díomhaoineach)

Éamann Ó Raghallaigh (Giúistís)

Beirt Shíothmhaor agus Tuilleadh

Beirt Fhear Dlí

Sa bhliain 1848 a tharla ábhar an dráma

ÁIT: Teach na Baintrí.

Siobhán agus Caitlín láithreach ag fuireach le Séamas a chuaigh in éineacht le mórán eile ag troid ar son a dtíre. Tá siad ag brath ar Chathair Chill Chainnigh a bhaint den bhurdún chosanta ghallda.

CAITLÍN *(.i. an iníon):* A mháthair, tá sé chomh maith dúinn an tine a choigilt. Níl aon mhaith a bheith ag fanacht le Séamas níos faide. Ní thiocfaidh sé anocht.

SIOBHÁN: Beimid buíoch má thagann sé choíche. Is caillte an scéal é agus gan aon mhac beo sa domhan agam ach é féin. *(Í ag gol).* Faraor géar, deacrach, nár cailleadh é an oíche ar rugadh é.

CAITLÍN: Stad, a mháthair, agus bíodh ciall agat.

SIOBHÁN: Ní fhéadaim, a Chaitlín. Tá mo chroí ag cuimhneamh air ó thosaigh sé ar an obair chlamprach seo.

CAITLÍN: Agus cén neart atá agat air? Nach gcaithfear é uair éigin? Agus nach bhfuil sé chomh maith dó bás a fháil ag troid go dúthrachtach in aghaidh deargnamhaid ár dtíre dúchais le bás a fháil leis an ocras ar leataobh an bhóthair? Tá a fhios agat go mbeidh an báille agus a chuid lorgairí bradacha anseo seachtain ón lá inniu agus beimid ón lá sin amach gan teach gan amhras agus cleith os ár gcionn ach cead againn a bheith ag breathnú ar réalta na spéire!

SIOBHÁN: Má thagann an saol go críoch orainn, dar ndóigh, tá Teach na mBocht againn le dul ann. Chualas go ndearnadh ceann de na tithe úd i nGaillimh le gairid.

CAITLÍN: Ar son Dé, a mháthair, ná labhair ar Theach na mBocht. Duine ar bith a rachadh isteach ansin faoi láthair, fanfaidh sé ann go dtiocfaidh sé amach sa gcónra.

SIOBHÁN: Tá daoine ansin a rugadh agus a tógadh chomh maith leatsa agus caithfidh siad fulaingt.

CAITLÍN: Chuile dhuine ar a bhealach féin. B'fhearr leo bás a fháil cois claí ná dul isteach ann.

Smaoiníonn Caitlín.

SIOBHÁN: Cé air a bhfuil tú ag smaoineamh, a chailín?

CAITLÍN: Tá mé ag cuimhneamh ar an ngéarleanúint atá muid a fháil ón rialtas gallda mallaithe seo. Is mó an troime atá acu sa bheithíoch ná sa Ghaeilge. Nach brónach an scéal é na daoine á ruaigeadh amach mar a bheadh préacháin ann as a gcuid talún a shaothraigh siad go crua agus bulláin agus caoirigh á seoladh go tiubh ina n-áit.

SIOBHÁN: B'fhéidir dá scríobhadh duine éigin litir chuig Landers nach mbeadh sé chomh dian sin orainn.

CAITLÍN: Ó, go bhfóire Dia ort! Scríobh Mánas na leabhar, an scríbhneoir is cliste sa bparóiste a bhí ina mháistir scoile fadó agus is éard a rinne Landers an litir a dhó sa tine gan a léamh ar chor ar bith.

SIOBHÁN: Ó, an bithiúnach! Nach beag an faitíos atá air roimh Dhia!

CAITLÍN: Faitíos roimh Dhia airsean! Is mó go mór an faitíos ba cheart dó a bheith air roimh an diabhal.

SIOBHÁN: Tá an-eagla orm go gcasfar Séamas leis agus má chastar déanfar ár.

CAITLÍN: Go deimhin, ní dhéanfar. Ní ghortódh Séamas ribe gruaige ar a cheann.

SIOBHÁN: Is deacair sin a dhéanamh mar nach bhfuil aon ghruaig air. Más fíor do Pháidín Rua é, thit gach uile ribe gruaige a bhí ar a cheann an oíche tar éis Brídín Ní Chinnéide a chur amach ar an mbóthar.

CAITLÍN: An í sin an bhean bhocht a thóg sé ar leaba an bháis lena cur amach?

SIOBHÁN: An bhean chéanna. Bhí sí chomh dona sin nár mhair sí ach uair an chloig ina dhiaidh sin.

Torann ag an doras.

CAITLÍN: Éist! B'fhéidir gurb é Séamas atá ann. Ní hé ar m'anam ach Dónall Diaganta agus nárb é a bheatha.

Téann Dónall isteach.

DÓNALL: Bail ó Dhia agus ó Mhuire, ó na naoimh agus ó na haingil oraibh.

CAITLÍN: Ó, 'sé do bheatha, a Dhónaill, suigh síos.

DÓNALL: Go raibh maith agat, a Shiobhán. Cogar, ar tháinig scéal ar bith ó Shéamas fós?

SIOBHÁN: Níor tháinig scéal anseo, ach fuair Bríd Ní Choirín scéal go raibh seisean agus a Pádraig féin ag oibriú go tréan faoin mBrianach.

DÓNALL: Dar fia! Is ait é an Brianach. Bhíos féin tamall agus mo phíce in mo láimh agam mar gach duine agus bheadh sé agam anois chomh maith ach gur cheapas go mba mhór an trua gan corrdhuine ag fanacht sa mbaile chun breathnú i ndiaidh na gcréatúr bocht atá á gcur amach. Ó, dá bhfeicfeá na páistí beaga ag screadach, chuirfeadh sé trua ar an Turcach is cruachroíoch a chonaic tú riamh. (*É ag smaoineamh*). Ach má tá drochscéal agam, a Shiobhán, nílim gan dea-scéal a chuirfeas áthas ar do chroí.

SIOBHÁN: Ára, cén scéal é, a Dhónaill?

DÓNALL: Bás Captaen Landers. Maraíodh ar maidin inniu é le piostal. D'inseoinn duit i dtosach é ach deirtear nach cóir drochscéal mar é siúd a insint go suíonn duine síos ar chor ar bith.

SIOBHÁN: Ó, más ea, a Dhónaill, sháraigh tú an méid a chonaic mé riamh. Anois díreach dúirt tú gur dea-scéal a bhí ann!

DÓNALL: Ó! Tá sé go maith agus go holc. Is maith an scéal duitse agus domsa é ach is dona an scéal é dá mhuintir féin.

SIOBHÁN: Níor inis tú dúinn cén chaoi ar éirigh sé dó.

DÓNALL: Simplí go leor. Is amhlaidh a bhí sé ina chóiste mór agus é ag imeacht ar rothaí an tsaoil mar a déarfá nuair a fuair sé piléar sa chúl a chuir deireadh lena shaol.

CAITLÍN: B'fhéidir gur óna lámha féin a tháinig an piléar.

DÓNALL: Deamhan fios cén chaoi ar éirigh sé dó. Níl mise ag insint ach an rud a chualas féin.

SIOBHÁN: Go ndéana Dia trócaire air ar chuma ar bith! Cé go raibh sé go holc.

CAITLÍN: Áiméan, más cóir é a rá!

DÓNALL: Tá cáil orm féin a bheith níos diaganta ná fear ar bith eile sa pharóiste: ach deirimse libh gur fada a bheinn ag paidreáil *(guí)* go gcuirfinn paidir lena anam. Trócaire don bhithiúnach úd go deimhin! Is iomaí baintreach agus dílleachta a d'iarr trócaire air féin agus ba bheag an mhaith dóibh sin. Chaith sé amach ar an mbóthar iad mar a chaithfeadh sé mada. *(Féachann sé thart timpeall an tí).* Tabhair deoch dom, a Shiobhán, má tá sí in do sheilbh, táim spalltha leis an tart.

SIOBHÁN: Go deimhin, a Dhónaill, is dona a bheadh an saol orm an lá nach mbeadh deoch agam duitse. Is fadó a thairgeoinn duit í ach baineadh geit bheag asam nuair a chualas faoi bhás Landers agus rinneas dearmad ar an digh.

DÓNALL: Go lige Dia slán thú, a Shiobhán! Dá mbeadh an domhan caillte nach gcaithfimid maireachtáil?

Ólann sé an deoch.

Go lige Dia slán an mháithreach! Gorta ná anachain ná imní na bliana nár fheice tú ag do dhoras choíche agus go bhfaighe tú bua ar do namhaid!

SIOBHÁN: Go mb'amhlaidh duit, a Dhónaill. Ach cogar. Measann tú an bhfaighfear spás beag aimsire anois mar gheall ar bhás Landers?

DÓNALL: B'fhéidir go bhfaighfí agus b'fhéidir nach bhfaighfí. Caithfidh an dlí dul ar aghaidh dá mb'éigean don chat a dhul sa ngarraí dá gabhainn. Ach geallaim go ndéanfaidh mise mo dhícheall duit ar chuma ar bith.

SIOBHÁN: Go mba slán, saolach an scéalaí! Ach tá faitíos orm gur beag é do dhícheall leis an mbáille nó le fear na bpróiseanna nó leis an tiarna talún ach an oiread liom féin.

DÓNALL: Cá bhfios duit?

SIOBHÁN: Tá a fhios agam é. Fear ar bith a thóg airm in aghaidh an rialtais!

DÓNALL: Ó ná bac leis sin. Mura ndéana mise cúis, gheobhaidh mé duine éigin eile a dhéanfas duit é. Tá an príomhbháille agus mo dheartháir, Seán, chomh mór le chéile le beirt ghadaí capaill. Rud ar bith a d'iarrfadh Seán air dá mb'éigean don bháille a dhul síos go dtína mhuineál sa loch dá sholáthar tá sé le fáil aige. Ach ná raibh maith ar a shon sin aige. Murach Seán, bheadh an deargbhithiúnach anois ag deargadh a sheandúidín lena mhéar.

SIOBHÁN: Céard a rinne Seán go mbeadh oibleagáid chomh mór sin ag an mbáille air?

DÓNALL: Seo é an chaoi ar thit sé amach. Bhí buíon mhór fear agus púicíní orthu ag tóraíocht an bháille oíche áirithe, tá coicís ó shin, le séaras breá de phúdar agus piléir a thabhairt dó. Nuair a rugadar air rinne Micheál Óg Ó Laoidhigh iarracht ar bheart próiseanna a sháitheadh síos trína sheanscornach agus thachtfaí é an uair úd murach Seán a bheith láithreach. Tá súil agam anois go gcoinneoidh tú an rún sin agat féin. *(Leis féin).* Ó nach simplí mé ag iarraidh ar mhnaoi rún a choinneáil! Ach, cén dochar? Is cuma liom cé a chloisfeas an méid sin.

SIOBHÁN: Tá faitíos orm go bhfuil sé deireanach anois – go bhfuil an díobháil déanta cheana.

DÓNALL: Má tá, níl sé níos déanaí ná an lá inné ó fuair Seán litir ón bpríomhbháille. Dúirt an báille gur le maith a dhéanamh don tír atá na tiarnaí talún ag cur na dtionóntaí amach – go bhfuil an iomarca daoine sa tír ar fad.

SIOBHÁN: Tá an iomarca drochdhaoine an lá a bhfuil seisean ann ar chuma ar bith.

DÓNALL: Tá dhá mhilliún airgid gearrtha amach i mbliana le haghaidh an tír seo a fheabhsú agus deir sé go rachaidh a bhunáite sin mar chostas chun na daoine bochta a ruaigfear amach a chur anonn go dtí na hIndiacha Thiar nó pé ar bith ceard den domhan ina bhfuil siad le cur ag triall. Ba mhaith leo, a deir sé, gach duine beag agus mór atá in ann a bheatha a shaothrú a dhíbirt as an tír – chuile dhuine ach an bacach nó an cláiríneach nó an seanduine atá rólag le obair a dhéanamh. Caithfidh a leithéidí sin, ár ndóigh, a dhul isteach go Teach na mBocht.

SIOBHÁN: An áit a rachaidh mise, tá faitíos orm.

DÓNALL: Deamhan baol ort, le cúnamh Dé. Ní fhágfaidh tú an teach seo go bhfaighe tú bás. Anois tóg suas do chroí is bíodh misneach agat.

SIOBHÁN: Mise mo bhannaí nach dtug sé aon mhisneach dúinn ins an litir sin.

DÓNALL: Thug agus ní thug. Dúirt sé go raibh sé féin in aghaidh sibh a chur amach ar chor ar bith ach nach bhfuil an tiarna talún sásta gan an dá ghabháltas .i. do ghabháltas-sa agus gabháltas Mháirtín Uí Eidhin a bheith in aon ghabháltas amháin. Ach cá bhfuil an tiarna talún anois? Tá sé imithe agus a mhaoin shaolta go léir fágtha ina dhiaidh aige.

SIOBHÁN: Má tá sé imithe féin nach mbeidh an méid a bhí ina sheilbh ag a dheartháir? 'Dá dhonacht maol is measa mullach'. Ach, dá ndéanadh sé a dhícheall, dheamhan a bhféadfadh Landers Óg a bheith níos measa ná an Caiptín!

CAITLÍN: De réir na cáile atá air ní bheidh sé níos fearr.

SIOBHÁN *(Go brónach):* Ó, ní bheidh. Is éard a dhéanfas sé an dá ghabháltas a thabhairt do Mháirtín agus sinn a fhágáil gan fód ar bith.

CAITLÍN: Tá amhras orm go raibh lámh ag Máirtín féin ann, mar rinne sé casaoid leis an Máistir anuraidh (is é sin an Máistir a bhí) go raibh an claí atá eadrainn ró-íseal agus dá bharr sin go mbíodh an bhodóg agus na gamhna beaga ag dul isteach air.

DÓNALL: Ó, ní raibh ansin ach leithscéal. Nárbh fhurasta dó an claí a ardú? Pé ar bith rud a dúirt Máirtín d'fhéadfadh an báille 'focal sa chúirt' a chur isteach duitse. Tá súil agam gur aige a fhágfar socrú na cúise ar fad. Céard atá aige le déanamh ansin ach bréag a chumadh ar Mháirtín – a rá leis an oidhre óg go raibh Mac Uí Eidhin ag cúlchaint air – gur dhúirt sé seo agus siúd leis – *(ag bualadh a uchta)*. Ó, go maithe Dia dom é! ionas go mb'fhéidir gurbh é Máirtín féin a chuirfí amach agus go bhfágfaí an dá ghabháltas agatsa.

SIOBHÁN: Nílimid ag iarraidh ach ár gcuid féin a fhágáil againn. Nílimid chomh santach sin is go mbeadh dúil againn seilbh a thógáil ar chuid ár gcomharsan.

Téann Tadhg Ó Dubháin, seoinín suarach, isteach.

SIOBHÁN: Ó, céad fáilte, a Thaidhg.

TADHG: Go maire tú, a Shiobhán.

DÓNALL *(Leis féin):* Diabhal mórán fáilte agamsa roimhe! Nach orm a bhí an tubaiste nach ndearnas mo ghnó sular tháinig sé isteach.

TADHG: Is cosúil nár tháinig Séamas fós.

SIOBHÁN: Níor tháinig agus tá an-imní orm faoi.

TADHG: Chualas urchair gunnaí á gcaitheamh ansin thuas. Níor shíleas go raibh an comhrac chomh gar sin dúinn.

DÓNALL: An bhfuil faitíos ort?

TADHG: Níl mé saor.

DÓNALL: Is cosúil gurb é sin an fáth ar tháinig tú isteach.

TADHG: Ní hé ar fad. Theastaigh uaimse cúpla focal eile a rá léi. Ach tiomáin leat. Ní bheidh mise in mo chónaí. Feicfidh tú féin. *(Tosaíonn sé ag scríobh le peann luaidhe).*

TADHG *(Le Siobhán):* Is éard a bhí mé ag brath ar a rá, a Shiobhán, dá mbeinn anseo sular imigh Séamas go ndéanfainn iarracht ar a choinneáil agus go gcuirfinn ar bhealach a leasa é.

SIOBHÁN: Go raibh maith agat, a Thaidhg. Ach cén mhaith duitse a bheith ag iarraidh a choinneáil an lá ar theip sé ar a mháthair a thug cíoch dó?

TADHG: Chuirfinnse smaoineamh ina cheann nach bhfuil a fhios agatsa ar chor ar bith, b'fhéidir.

SIOBHÁN: Agus cén sórt smaointe é sin, le do thoil?

TADHG: Chuirfinn faoi ndeara dó pósadh agus chuirfinn rud beag céille ina chloigeann aerach.

SIOBHÁN: Lig dom, a Thaidhg, ní pósadh a bhí ag cur imní air.

TADHG: Tá a fhios agamsa céard a bhí ag cur imní air. Theastaigh airgead uaidh chun an cíos a íoc agus nuair a chonaic sé céard a bhí i ndán dó thóg sé an claíomh agus d'imigh sé leis i ndiaidh a chinn roimhe.

SIOBHÁN: Agus cé a bhéarfadh dó é, má theastaigh airgead uaidh?

TADHG: Bhéarfaidh mise dó é agus rud níos fearr ná sin .i. bean chomh ciallmhar, chomh tíosach agus atá sa pharóiste.

SIOBHÁN: An í do dheirfiúr atá i gceist agat?

TADHG: Is í, a mh'ainín.

SIOBHÁN: Shíleas go raibh sí féin agus Mcheál Ó Dochartaigh óstóir le pósadh roimh an gCarghas seo chugainn.

[NÍ CRÍOCH]